Controlling the Federal Bureaucracy

Controlling the Federal Bureaucracy

Dennis D. Riley

Temple University Press   *Philadelphia*

Temple University Press, Philadelphia 19122
Copyright © 1987 by Temple University. All rights reserved
Published 1987
Printed in the United States of America

Library of Congress Cataloging-in-Publication Data

Riley, Dennis D.
    Controlling the federal bureaucracy.
    Bibliography: p. 189
    Includes index.
    1. Administrative agencies — United States.
2. Bureaucracy — United States.   3. United States —
Politics and government.   I. Title.
JK421.R52   1987   353.07′5   86-14469
ISBN 0-87722-455-2 (alk. paper)

The paper used in this publication meets the minimum
requirements of American National Standard for Information
Sciences — Permanence of Paper for Printed Library Materials,
ANSI Z39.48-1984

To Katy and Annie, I love you

Contents

Preface

How do we fit a powerful bureaucracy into a democratic political system? The list of people who have addressed that question would make a pretty good inaugural class for a Public Administration Hall of Fame. Herman Finer and Carl Friedrich exchanged heated words over the subject nearly half a century ago. In the years following World War II, Paul Appleby, Arthur Maass, and Dwight Waldo made important contributions to the debate, and the next two decades brought Stephen Bailey, Frederick Mosher, Roscoe Martin, Emmette Redford, Herbert Kaufman, and Francis Rourke into the circle of scholars searching for some path toward a bureaucracy governed by democratic values.

Though some of those scholars put more faith in one method than the other, all pretty much agree that we must both try to convince bureaucrats they ought to tread the democratic path (an internal check) and make it extremely difficult for them to get off that path should they try (an external check). The purpose of this little book is to examine the state of those external checks. That is, are there barriers, set up by other institutions, that prevent bureaucrats from straying too far from the democratic straight and narrow? Or, to put it in a bit more straightforward way, does anybody outside the bureaucracy have the ability to influence what bureaucrats do, and if the answer is Yes, who is it and do they use their influence to promote the values of democracy?

In the study of government—and a lot of other things as well, I suspect—the fun questions don't have clear-cut answers. These are no exception. Still, we can be relatively certain that there are outsiders who do influence what happens inside the executive branch of the federal government.

Key members and staff personnel of the congressional committees and subcommittees with jurisdiction over a particular agency have a great deal to say about what happens at that agency. So do the leaders—and the lobbyists—of that agency's clientele groups and those chosen to represent the associations of professionals or subject matter experts concerned with this agency's policy area. There are even a handful of individual policy experts who are consistently in on the act. These three sets of people have a good bit of influence and each uses it to advance its own interests, which just happen to coincide with those of the other two almost all of the time, and which all three—and their agency—define as the public interest.

Three other sets of people—the President and his people, the courts, and individuals and groups who devote their lives to criticizing bureaucracy—have some influence, too. It is far less pervasive and it often irritates bureaucrats to no end, but it is there. Most of the time the President pays little attention to the goings on in the federal bureaucracy and he is ill equipped to try to lead that bureaucracy in new directions, but if he is angry about what a particular agency is doing and he is willing to put up a fight, he can be a formidable foe. Courts enter the bureaucratic arena only when invited by someone else, which isn't all that often, but when they do they can have quite an impact. Finally, groups like the Sierra Club and the Wilderness Society, or the various Ralph Nader spin-offs like Critical Mass, spend their time harassing the agencies that deal with the issues they care about. The President, the courts, and the critics do not achieve anything like the day-to-day influence of congressional subcommittees, clientele groups, and professional associations, but they are felt nonetheless. Even when they are felt, it can be extremely difficult to assess the impact of their influence. Is the President really the tribune of all the people? Do the courts see individual rights and liberties with unerring accuracy? Can Ralph Nader really see the general public interest when everyone else sees only the special interests? Still, their impact may be every bit as likely to push us in democratic directions as is the impact of the subcommittees and the rest of bureaucracy's allies. Maybe more.

It is hard to say exactly when and where this book originated. In some sense it started in the early 1960's when Ed Stillings got me interested in public administration and convinced me I could be a college professor. The mid-1960's and graduate study with Roscoe Martin, and, for one week, with Emmette Redford, turned the interest in public administration to a more specific concern with the questions of how to fit bureaucracy into our democratic governing system. Three years with Jack Walker at the University of Michigan sharpened my research skills and centered my attention on the role of bureaucrats in policy making. So, thanks to all of you for getting me started.

The actual writing of the book began in the summer of 1981. I got a lot of help from a lot of people as the writing progressed. Ed Miller of my department here always seemed to have the book or article I didn't have, and sometimes had the book or article I didn't even know existed. Other departmental colleagues, especially John Morser and Mark Cates, listened to ideas in which they had only a marginal interest and, more importantly, created the kind of environment in which I work best—noisy and disorganized. Two reviewers whose names I do not know helped immeasurably. The first read a very early draft for a commercial publisher. The book was rejected, but this reviewer offered all kinds of first-rate suggestions and I incorporated most of them. One of Temple's own reviewers also helped a great deal with suggestions on overall organization and especially with the chapter on the President and his relationship with the bureaucracy. Finally, our department secretary, Rita Klismith, went beyond the traditional role of typist and became teacher. I actually learned word processing—enough of it to do the manuscript, with some help—and then she turned the disks into real printed pages. She still claims it isn't magic.

I have saved the three most important thank-yous of all for last. Jane Cullen at Temple University Press had faith in a first-time author, and I owe her a lot for that. Doris Braendel, Temple's managing editor, saved me from the embarrassment of countless little goofs—and a handful of real blunders—while leaving a book that still sounds and feels like me. How much would an author pay for such an editor? But the biggest debt of all is the one I owe my friend and colleague Jeff Olen. Jeff writes—a lot. He writes well. He convinced me that I, too, could write and he propped me up every time I tried to quit. Then when I had pretty much given up, he told me to call Jane. I didn't, but he knew me well enough to know that, so he did. Jane called me and a manuscript finally became a book. Thanks, Jeff, for everything.

Dennis D. Riley
Stevens Point, Wisconsin
May 1986

Controlling the Federal Bureaucracy

Introduction

On December 29, 1970, the Congress and the President promised the men and women of America's industrial work force safe and healthy places to work. Keeping that promise meant determining how much cotton dust the air of a textile factory could contain before breathing that air became dangerous. It meant being certain that safety guards were installed on machines that could sever a limb in a split second. It meant inspecting thousands of work sites looking for noise, dust, chemicals, dangerous machinery, poorly designed work processes, even careless workers. And it meant offering suggestions for improvement, issuing citations for failure to change, and assessing fines for repeated violations.

Because keeping the promise of a safe and healthy work environment requires all of these things, Congress and the President can only make the promise. They cannot keep it. They lack the technical knowledge to set the standards and the bodies to do the inspections. So they hire them; that is, they create an organization —in this case, the Occupational Safety and Health Administration—and tell that organization to get the requisite combination of bodies and knowledge and put that combination to use keeping the promise of safe and healthy work places.

Every time the President and Congress feel the need to make another promise, they have to create one more organization. Safe skies mean the Federal Aviation Administration. Safe and effective prescription drugs mean the Food and Drug Administration. The right of workers to bargain collectively about wages, hours, and working conditions means the National Labor Relations Board, the effort to provide some sort of economic security for farmers means the Agricultural Stabilization and Conservation Service, and the goal of making the Interior West a region of farms means the Bureau of Reclamation.

Each individual promise demands an agency. Pile two hundred years of promises one on top of the other, and you have bureaucracy.

The Need to Control Bureaucracy

Bureaucracy is inevitable all right, but that doesn't help us figure out what to make of it. Should we love it? Hate it? Should we be afraid of it? Or should we just ignore it?

It's hard to imagine loving bureaucracy, but remember, every agency exists to fulfill some sort of promise and politicians made those promises because they were convinced some of us wanted to hear them. Each trip to the pharmacy reminds me that the Food and Drug Administration has agreed that amoxycillin fights certain bacteria and is safe for a kid with an ear infection, and even promises that this particular batch is OK. I may not exactly love the FDA, but I'm glad it's there. Farmers probably feel the same way about the Agricultural Stabilization and Conservation Service, frequent air travelers about the Federal Aviation Administration, and Great Lakes and coastal boaters about the Coast Guard.

It's a whole lot easier to imagine hating bureaucracy. Perhaps hate is too strong a word. Still, not an issue of *Reader's Digest* goes by without some gleeful bureaucracy bashing, and it isn't easy remembering the last time a prominent politician launched into a vigorous defense of career civil servants and the rules they write or the services they provide. To be sure, individual politicians defend individual agencies, but from the top on down, elected officials rail against the amorphous enemy, The Bureaucracy. Jimmy Carter used this sort of public hostility toward bureaucracy as a key ingredient in his drive for the White House, and Ronald Reagan not only succeeded in using it to oust Carter, but somehow managed to keep his anti-bureaucratic image intact throughout his first term and on through a second campaign. Not a bad trick for someone whose title is Chief Executive.

Whether we hate bureaucracy or not, there are some of us who fear it. Some people fear it because of what it could do to them. Bureaucracy can lose checks, send checks for the wrong amount, or declare that you no longer deserve a check at all, causing immense economic and psychological hardship in the process. It can write rules that reduce the value of your property, levy fines, issue and revoke licenses, and do hundreds of other things that directly affect millions of lives. Others of us, especially in my profession, fear it on a different level. Democracy is based on a presumption that the people ought to be in control of their own government. At a minimum, that means they must have a say in who runs that government and periodic opportunities to approve or disapprove of the way they are running it. By no stretch of the imagination can anyone conclude that we have that sort of chance to say Yes or No to the people and policies of OSHA, The FDA, or the Soil Conservation Service. That scares a lot of us, and it should.

Finally, of course, most of the time most of us don't love bureaucracy, or hate it, or fear it; we just ignore it. Unless we bump up against a particular agency on a particular question we are hardly aware of bureaucracy's existence.

Whatever we feel about bureaucracy, there is one reaction we all share. We want to control it. We want to be able to influence what it does with the power we are forced to give it. Those who love it want to make sure it keeps on doing the things that make them happy. Those who hate it almost inevitably want to keep it from doing much of anything. Those who fear it on a personal level want to prevent it from harming them and those of us who fear it on a more abstract level want to find a way to make it fit into our already messy governmental structure without doing violence to our basic values.

In specific instances, the ends to which this influence will be put may be anything from holding on to a valuable broadcast license to protecting battered women and children. In general, however, the end is democracy itself. Somehow we all want a bureaucracy that responds to the thoughts and feelings of a majority of citizens, takes care not to violate the rights of the individuals with which it deals, and shows some extra concern for the strongly held feelings of whatever segment of the population it is called upon to serve and/or regulate.

Majority rule, individual rights, and responsiveness to intense minorities hardly exhausts the list of democratic values that we want to have guide bureaucratic policy making, but even if we add to the list for pages, the question remains, how can we get them to do it? To no one's surprise, we have been offered two answers: convince them they ought to (an internal check), and show them they have to (an external check).

Bureaucrats are human beings, products of a democratic culture and tied to professional and public service ethics. John Gaus and Carl Friedrich concluded half a century ago that this immersion in professional commitments and democratic culture would serve as a powerful check on bureaucrats tempted to stray from the democratic straight and narrow.[1] Francis Rourke must still believe this kind of check is possible, for the following assertion has survived three editions of his widely read and highly influential *Bureaucracy, Politics, and Public Policy* intact: "Perhaps the best kind of 'inner check' upon bureaucratic power is not interagency rivalry, which requires, after all, a vigorously competitive relationship between two or more executive organizations, but restraints that operate within the personalities of bureaucrats themselves, preventing them from unlawful or excessive use of the power placed in their keeping."[2]

Not everyone agrees that bureaucrats can be made to see the democratic light, however. Herman Finer registered a vigorous dissent from the Gaus-Friedrich view in his now famous "Administrative Responsibility in Democratic Government."[3] With an avowedly Rousseauian belief that the people cannot be wrong (merely unwise), Finer argued that "while reliance on an official's conscience may be reliance on an official's accomplice, in democratic administration all parties, . . . will breathe easier if a censor is in the offing."[4] Though less prone to express their distrust of individual bureaucrats with the vigor displayed by Finer, Arthur Maass and Emmette Redford argued for strong external controls on bureaucracy as an absolutely essential ingredient in twentieth century democracy.[5]

The line between internal checks and external controls is nowhere near as easy to draw as the preceding paragraphs probably implied, and even if one could draw it with confidence, Friedrich, Finer, Maass, Redford, and Rourke would almost certainly be found straddling it anyway. All of these men, as well as Dwight Waldo, Roscoe Martin, Frederick and William Mosher, and the dozens of other scholars who have devoted their lives to trying to fit bureaucracy into the framework of a democratic system, recognized that neither the internal check nor all the external controls imaginable could do the job alone. The Congress, the President, the courts, and the public cannot possibly monitor the activities of more than a million highly specialized professionals and there is no way that we could recruit a million-plus policy specialists each equipped with a fully developed democratic conscience and an unerring feel for the public pulse. Getting bureaucracy on the democratic path requires a commitment from inside the bureaucrat and some reinforcement from H. L. Mencken's version of conscience, that little voice telling us that someone is watching.

Bureaucracy Is Just Bureaucrats

The bureaucracy that we seek to control is anything but an inert mass waiting for direction. It is a handful of Cabinet departments — which turn out to be loosely related collections of semi-autonomous bureaus often containing stubbornly independent subdivisions of their own—with some independent agencies no one has yet been able to force into one of the departments and the various regulatory commissions thrown in for good measure. Each of these hundreds of bureaucratic subunits has a unique mission and its own political and organizational history and woe to the outsider who tries to control any of them without a pretty detailed knowledge of both.[6] But, most of all, that bureaucracy we worry so much about is a collection of individuals. Each comes carrying his or her own intellectual and emotional baggage and that baggage will have a significant impact on how he or she reacts to outside efforts at control.

The Bureaucrat as Policy Specialist

It takes a lot of people to keep the promise of workplace safety, and, as a group anyway, these people have to possess a rather wide range of knowledge. Some of that knowledge—knowing enough to put No Smoking signs near gasoline, for instance—is only a step or two removed from common sense. But some of it—say, whether that particular machine is dangerous or how much benzene in the air of a factory is too much—is pretty technical. Most of us don't know and probably don't even know how to find such information. But OSHA needs to know, so it needs to hire people who can find out. Most of these people have completed university degrees in safety engineering or industrial hygiene. Many of the rest are chemists, biologists, or public health professionals with specialized training relevant to the questions of industrial safety. Years of specialized training plus on-the-job experience lead these people to develop pretty strong feelings about how to make factories safer. The most powerful of these feelings is the conviction that the knowledge they have ought to be the primary determinant of industrial safety policy.

Precisely the same sort of belief prevails among all sorts of other policy specialists at all sorts of agencies. Foresters believe that the use of our timber resources must be guided by sound forest management principles, principles that they just happen to understand and that the rest of us probably can't quite grasp. The doctors and pharmacologists at the FDA see themselves as the only ones able to design and implement a system for approving new drugs, just as the lawyers at the Federal Trade Commission's Bureau of Competition feel that they have the key to sound anti-trust policy. The fact that the economists at the FTC's Bureau of Economics are convinced that they have the key and that it is a completely different key fazes neither the lawyers nor the economists.[7]

Even after they have long since moved into executive positions, a good many career bureaucrats continue to identify more strongly with their chosen specialties than with their roles as administrators. The Senior Executive Service is a group that most of us think of as managers, yet Frederick Mosher found that within that managerial elite people who had "made or participated in decisions affecting thousands of subordinates, millions of citizens, and sometimes billions of dollars . . . still thought of themselves as engineers, biologists, lawyers, economists."[8]

When a particular policy specialty belongs to a recognized profession, this identification/commitment becomes all the stronger, for now it is reinforced by the profession's status, its ability to determine how many folks will be allowed into the fraternity and what they must do to join, the tendency of its members to internalize the profession's ideology and code of ethics, and society's willingness to allow most professions to police themselves with little if any outside interference.[9] When a recognized profession dominates a policy specialty and that specialty is central to the mission of a particular agency, we can easily reach the point at which "the goals and standards of public agencies, as seen by their officers and employees, are identical with the goals and standards of the professions as they are seen by their members."[10] Why not? They are pretty much the same people.

In a sense, belief in specialized knowledge, especially one's own, is almost a twentieth-century religion. Nowhere is its hold on individual bureaucrats better expressed than in these words form Frederick Mosher: "Professionalism rests upon specialized knowledge, science, and rationality. There are *correct* ways of solving problems and doing things. Politics [and politicians no doubt] is seen as being engaged in the fuzzy areas of negotiation, elections, votes, compromises—*all carried on by subject matter amateurs*. Politics is to the professions as ambiguity to truth, expediency to rightness, heresy to true belief."[11]

Mosher's last sentence may take a wee bit of poetic license, but it captures the spirit of the approach to industrial safety policy that predominates among the career staff of the Occupational Safety and Health Administration. OSHA is pretty much the province of men and women with graduate, or at least undergraduate, training in safety engineering or industrial hygiene. The values of both branches of the occupational safety profession are strongly pro-protection. The National Safety Council manual tells future safety engineers that they must do all they can to prevent industrial accidents since "failure to take necessary precautions against predictable accidents involves moral responsibility for those accidents."[12] The extent to which they take the manual to heart is evidenced by Steven Kelman's observation that "I have frequently been struck by hearing safety professionals utter expressions such as 'We killed ten workers when that scaffold collapsed' rather than saying, impersonally, 'Ten workers were killed.'[13]

Nowhere is the safety engineer's occupational ideology more on display than in the choice between personal protective equipment—ear plugs, masks, respirators, and the like—and engineering controls—reduced noise, gas or particulate levels in the work place and so on. Personal protective equipment is cheap. Engineering controls are not. But the safety engineer will almost always opt for controls. Every textbook he or she ever read warned against protective equipment. As Steven Kelman observes, "The textbooks imply that relying on personal protective equipment is seen as a confession of failure, a betrayal of the can-do approach of the engineer, a renunciation of pluck and determination, and a yielding to laziness and defeat. Personal protective equipment is visualized as a paste-over, a Band-Aid—indeed, a sort of industrial Potemkin village, a pleasing facade masking actual failure. As much as it may be unpleasant to the workers, *personal protective equipment is insulting to the engineer.*"[14] OSHA has fought each of the last three Presidents over the issue of safety equipment versus engineering controls and there is every reason to believe it will keep up the battle.

The Bureaucrat as Politician

Bureaucrats may firmly believe that knowledge ought to play the dominant role in the making of policy decisions, but they do concede some role to politics, that is, to the reaction a policy will generate among the people who know and care about it. They do so for two reasons.

First, of course, they cannot avoid it. They work for government. They are dependent on elected officials—politicians—for budgets, legal authority, even their very existence. Herbert Kaufman's observations of the activities of the six bureau chiefs he studied certainly apply to the vast majority of career administrators: "This set of congressional and congressionally related workers in the machinery of government seemed rarely to be out of the administrator's consciousness. The chiefs were constantly looking over their shoulders, as it were, at the elements of the legislative establishment relevant to their agencies—taking stock of moods and attitudes, estimating reactions to contemplated decisions and actions, trying to prevent misunderstandings and avoidable conflicts, and planning responses when storm warnings appeared on the horizon."[15]

Bureaucrats know they have to let politics in, but I believe they also feel they ought to. The evidence here is far less clear cut, but democracy is a powerful idea, socialization a powerful force. I may not be quite as convinced as Carl Friedrich and John Gaus were half a century ago that a democratic conscience can be found inside every bureaucrat. Still, Francis Rourke does make a pretty good case that public service and specific professional codes of ethics by their constant repetition of the need for "a subordinate role for bureaucrats in the governmental process" put considerable pressure on career public servants to accept the legitimacy of political forces in the policy process.[16]

Whether the decision be Social Security reform or the allowable level of benzene in factory air, that decision will be based in part on knowledge (the best guess of those people with information and the ability to interpret that information as to what policy will effectively address the problem at hand) and in part on politics (the best guess about the reaction to the decision of the people most likely to know and care about it). That's OK from a bureaucratic perspective, so long as the mix of knowledge and politics is appropriate. Ironically, the way to try to keep the mix to the bureaucratic taste is for bureaucrats to become politicians. They do, and that, too affects their reaction to external controls. As we shall see, they accept some in order to eliminate others.

The Bureaucrat as Person

Finally, bureaucrats are people. Somehow, somewhere along the line they acquire a perspective on the world and a set of values that influences every aspect of their lives. Sometimes that perspective or those values may significantly affect a bureaucrat's feelings about the issues and questions that face his or her agency.

As noted earlier, safety engineering programs do their best to inculcate a pro-protection "bias" in those who will carry forward the industrial safety mantle. The task of socialization is bound to be that much easier when the one being socialized is one of the many future professionals who "report having lost relatives in industrial accidents."[17]

Less directly personal, but not necessarily less relevant, is the impact of common background and heritage found in those departments and agencies that recruit from a narrow regional or socio-economic base. The Interior Department recruits a very high proportion of its career staff from the Interior West, the Agriculture Department from the small towns and rural areas of the West and Midwest with some Southerners thrown in.[18] This is only logical, of course, since it is people, programs, and policies, not the lure of the exciting life of the civil servant, that draws most people to government service. Westerners tend to distrust Easterners, especially those with any connection to banks or railroads, and to take a view of the land as a nearly infinite resource to be tamed, not a scarce one to be "locked up." Both of these feelings leave their mark on a variety of Interior Department land management policies. In a similar vein, small town and rural people tend to distrust big city folks, and to take seriously the notion of agriculture as a "way of life," not a sector of the economy. Their ideas, too, rub off on the policies they pursue.

The Agriculture and Interior Departments are probably extreme examples, and even they are not truly homogeneous. Besides, not all Westerners think alike and half a dozen farmers can easily produce seven or eight farm programs. Still, as Harold Seidman notes, agencies and departments do exhibit "distinctive colorations," these colorations are well known, and they have an impact on who seeks—and who gains—employment in particular bureaucracies.[19] Presidents even respect these traditions. Though a clearly disproportionate number of federal political executives count a big name prep school as alma mater, not one of those ex-preppies toiled at Agriculture or Interior.[20] They wouldn't "fit" and everyone involved seems to know it.

These personal influences are almost certainly less important than either the commitment to knowledge or the acceptance of politics. In a good many instances these ingredients may be impossible to separate in any case. Is a safety engineer so committed to controls because Uncle Harry died in a preventable accident or because of the textbooks, lectures, and films that bombarded him or her in graduate school? Is an Agriculture Department Supergrade so committed to producer-oriented policies because of the good old days in Emmetsburg or the training he or she got at Iowa State? Nonetheless, personal factors count and they are constantly reinforced by the homogeneity of an agency's staff. Controls are bound to seem less offensive to bureaucrats when they come from people with whom these bureaucrats are personally comfortable.

The Complete Bureaucrat

Bureaucrats are not so many Humpty Dumpties hopelessly fractured into professional, political, and personal pieces that no one can put back together again. Somehow they manage to pull these three forces back together into a more or less integrated approach to their jobs and, more to the point in terms of this book, to the efforts made to control them. Controls—influence is probably a more appropriate term—exercised by people similar to agency staff in background and values, and, most important of all, who share its commitment to expert knowledge, are acceptable. The influence of amateurs, of people out of tune with agency values, is not. Politics can throw a king-sized monkey wrench into these best-laid plans, but as this book unfolds you will see that it seldom does.

A Sneak Preview

It is clear that we need both internal and external checks on bureaucracy, but, as I have already mentioned, this book will confine itself to the efforts to control bureaucrats from the outside. It's pretty tough to get inside the heads of more than a million career civil servants, and in any case we have put most of our eggs in that external basket.

So this book will look at the President, the Congress, the courts, and the public itself and their individual and collective efforts to control bureaucracy. Specifically, what are the mechanisms of control available to them, how well do they work, and do they give us a bureaucracy whose performance is consistent with the values of democracy?

Bureaucracy and the President

Getting elected President earns a person the title Chief Executive. Unfortunately, the job comes with it. To be Chief Executive is to be obligated to try to exercise some control over the hundreds of agencies theoretically subject to your command. Every President comes to realize the importance of this far-flung empire. It can help him achieve his objectives, or it can frustrate and even embarrass him by its actions. Like it or not, as Richard Cole and David Caputo have argued, "all recent presidents have attempted some measure of bureaucratic control and direction." [1]

They've tried all right, but the enterprise faces three rather formidable obstacles. First, it is almost impossible for a President to mount anything even approaching a sustained effort since he rarely knows what is happening in the rest of government. In addition, bureaucrats are fearful of presidential influence and will resist it as hard as they can. Finally, the Chief just doesn't have the tools to be Chief; that is, he lacks the resources to overcome bureaucratic resistance to his efforts at control.

What's Going On Down There, Anyway?

Whether the Chief wants to stop an agency from doing something he finds objectionable or induce it to do things he finds desirable, he needs to have some idea of what that agency is or is not doing now. The odds that the President is aware of what is going on at most agencies are slim indeed.

It is said that in response to a question about something he considered a "minor administrative matter," Lyndon Johnson turned on a reporter and bellowed, "Why do you come and ask me, the leader of the Western World, a chickenshit question like that?"[2] Though other Presidents might have chosen more delicate language, in public at least, there can be little doubt that the question has occurred to every occupant of 1600 Pennsylvania Avenue. The vast majority of bureaucratic agencies are engaged in activities that most Presidents find just plain boring. In a world of important legislative battles and international crises, how does a Chief Executive generate much interest in leasing public lands for the grazing of cattle and sheep (Bureau of Land Management), enforcement of mine safety standards (Mine Safety and Health Administration), or regulations for private aircraft at busy metropolitan airports (Federal Aviation Administration)? This is not to say that these questions are intrinsically dull, or that no one could possibly be interested in all of them at once, only that it is unlikely that any President would, or even could, maintain a consistent interest in these and all of the other issues confronting the thousands of executive branch agencies every day.

To be sure, if we lose a hundred West Virginia coal miners the day before Thanksgiving, the President will become very interested in MSHA, just as he will want to know more about the FAA and "general aviation" if a small private plane collides with a 747 full of passengers. Still, in the normal run of events, a President will exhibit no more than a perfunctory interest in the vast majority of bureaucratic agencies and their daily activities, and the Chief, just like the rest of us, isn't likely to know much about things that don't interest him.

Lack of interest is not the only barrier to presidential information gathering. No Chief Executive could conceivably muster the specialized knowledge needed to effectively monitor the performance of the thousands of agencies supposedly under his direction. A President certainly need not possess the same level of technical expertise exhibited by the men and women of a particular agency in order to check on its performance, but armed with only a passing familiarity with the agency and its programs —the normal presidential situation—how is the Chief Executive even to know what he has found? How is he to evaluate the agency's claim that what he wants is impossible, and that only the agency's solution to the problem at hand will work? In his relationship with any specific agency, the President is, by definition, an amateur. In his relationship with the entire bureaucracy, amateur may be too generous a label.

This lack of knowledge will not automatically prevent a President from checking up on a particular agency, or from trying to change its actions if he finds them distasteful. But his amateur status will probably make him wary of the potential charge of substituting politics for knowledge and at least slow him down a little.

Finally, no President has enough time to play the oversight role effectively. The pressures on a President's time are enormous, indeed, almost impossible to comprehend. Everyone wants a share of the presidential day, and the names of the Israeli Ambassador and the Cherry Blossom Princess are just about as likely to be on the presidential appointment calendar for next Wednesday as are those of the Director of the Soil Conservation Service or the Administrator of the FAA. Even if a President were willing to delegate all of his ceremonial duties to the Vice-President and devote all of his work day to monitoring bureaucracy, there is simply not enough time in that day to keep track of all of the various agencies. No Chief Executive has ever tried, but none could succeed.

It is true, of course, that the President is not alone in his efforts to monitor bureaucracy. He has a fairly large White House staff, the resources of the Executive Office of the President, special presidential commissions, and his appointees in the various departments and bureaus, and they do expand considerably his time, knowledge, and interest in bureaucracy. But even with these extensions of the Chief's presence, discovering what the myriad of bureaus and agencies are doing and prodding them toward a presidentially determined course remains an almost impossible task.

In the first place, as Hugh Heclo has pointed out, the President faces a virtual Catch-22 in selecting the men and women to aid him in this endeavor. A properly certified and acceptable expert is one who is "recognized as knowledgeable about the substance of the issues . . . but not irretrievably identified with highly controversial positions."[3] Such a person can keep tabs on bureaucracy fairly effectively, but is hardly a presidential representative. On the other hand, the true believer—either in the President or his policies—is likely to be unacceptable to "those in the know."[4] In the end, unless a President can put together a team of subject matter experts able to understand what they see, but willing to incur the wrath of fellow professionals on behalf of "their Chief," he is doomed to a network for monitoring bureaucracy that is ineffective, non-presidential, or both.

Second, despite the fact that the institutionalized Presidency now includes thousands of individuals, it remains extremely difficult for these men and women to extend the presidential presence into the rest of the executive branch no matter how hard they try. In the words of Thomas Cronin, "There is a great residual of respect toward the Presidency both in Washington and in the federal agencies throughout the country. But this respect for what the President can do is predicated on the fact that the Presidential voice can be heard and believed as authentic, not just through second-level staff voices. Otherwise, federal civil servants feel that they must protect their 'rational' and 'professional' interests from White House interference."[5] A lower-echelon White House staff member or the Executive Director of a presidential study commission may claim to speak for the Chief, and the claim may be true, but it is a claim that is hard to evaluate—unless, of course, the Chief substantiates it—and bureaucrats are reluctant to accept that claim at face value until he does. This does not mean that the President must become directly and personally involved before bureaucracy can be moved, but it is true that despite the size and scope of the institutionalized Presidency, his reach into the executive domain is still seriously limited.

Even with the substantial resources of the institutionalized Presidency, the Chief Executive has a difficult time finding out what is going on in his ostensible domain. Time is always short, he may not understand what he sees, and, besides that, he doesn't always care. It is true that a President doesn't need to know everything going on in the executive branch to make himself and his policies felt, but he has to have some rough idea of what is happening now and how it differs from what he wants to see happening, and most agencies know that, when it comes to them and their particular policy area, the Chief almost surely doesn't.

Bureaucratic Resistance to the President

Bureaucratic resistance to presidential influence is pretty well known, to Presidents, to bureaucrats, and to anyone who studies either one. One of the best known of all the comments ever made about the Presidency was Harry Truman's doleful prediction about the fate soon to befall his successor: "He'll sit here and he'll say, 'Do this! Do that!' *And nothing will happen.* Poor Ike —it won't be a bit like the Army. He'll find it very frustrating."[6] Apparently Harry was right. As one Eisenhower aide told Richard Neustadt, "The President still feels that when he's decided something, that ought to be the end of it . . . and when it bounces back undone or done wrong, he tends to react with shocked surprise."[7] It is hard to imagine a more famous instance of bureaucratic resistance than the joint State-Defense Department decision to ignore not one but two orders from the Kennedy White House to remove Jupiter missiles from Turkey—unless, of course, one counts J. Edgar Hoover's decision to decline some "dirty tricks" assignments that led to the formation of Richard Nixon's White House Plumbers Unit. But, famous or not, every President has had to endure them.[8]

Bureaucrats don't resist out of sheer orneriness. The policy expert in them says that presidential intervention in agency decision making is almost always ill timed, poorly thought out, and " 'political' in the negative sense — that is, an attempt to change a decision in response to 'special interest' maneuvering."[9] If the expert in them says we don't want to listen, the politician says we don't have to. The Chief doesn't have the political and organizational resources to force us to go along.

It's not terribly difficult to figure out why the expert side of the bureaucrat would want to resist. Bureaucrats are subject matter specialists, highly knowledgeable and in the policy process for the long haul. The President and his people are just the opposite. Their knowledge ranges from unsophisticated to non-existent, and they rarely seem to look much past the next CBS—New York Times poll. These two kinds of folks just don't mix well.

Agency staff are careerists, in government and very likely in that particular agency. In contrast, the President and his cadre of political executives are short termers. Not one member of the original twelve-man team Richard Nixon introduced with such fanfare on national television in 1968 was still around when Air Force One took its last flight to San Clemente. In the five-and-one-half-year interim, Nixon had four Treasury Secretaries and three men served at the top of the Agriculture Department.

This transience, particularly at the sub-Cabinet level, where the door revolves even faster, is annoying to career bureaucrats for two reasons. In the first place, two Deputy Secretaries, even if appointed by the same President and serving under the same Secretary, may have different approaches to a particular agency and its programs. If an agency has been responsive to one Deputy Secretary, it may find itself in trouble with his or her successor, and, in any event, even if trouble does not ensue, to be responsive to the next one may require a quick shift in policy direction. Experts are rarely fond of a zigzag course. Right answers, as defined by their expert knowledge, just don't change that fast. In addition, because they are permanent and their "superiors" temporary, agency staff feel that they will be the ones left holding the bag for unpopular policies designed by now-departed superiors. It is bad enough to take the heat. It is a whole lot worse when someone else made the decision and isn't here to take his or her share.

Transience may be an annoying characteristic of the President and his political executives, but their lack of expertise is downright galling. To return to Mosher's argument outlined in the previous chapter, the essence of professionalism is the belief in knowledge and every bureaucrat knows that the Chief and his team know less about that bureaucrat's bailiwick than he or she does. How could it be otherwise with 2,500 or so representing the President and trying to worry about a million plus? Because these people do not/cannot know what must be known to make intelligent policy choices, their influence has to be limited as much as possible, so the bureaucrat decides to resist.

The politician to be found in every bureaucrat believes resistance is possible—in fact, that it is very likely to succeed. I'll talk about the reasons—that is, about why the President can't push bureaucracy around—in the rest of the chapter. Before I do that, however, I should issue two notes of caution about bureaucratic resistance to the President.

First of all, the term resistance probably implies some presidential initiative that bureaucrats must counter. That happens seldom. Presidential inattention is the rule for most agencies, so, in effect, those agencies are merely reciprocating, that is, ignoring him more than resisting him. Second, when bureaucrats do resist, the classic—and definitely preferred—mode is passive resistance. Simply do not act. The odds of follow-up are extremely low, and even a second call can probably be ignored. At least that was the consensus of fifty former White House aides from three administrations.[10] Standing toe to toe with the President and slugging it out makes headlines, but it doesn't happen often.

If we interpret the notion of resistance broadly enough to include simply ignoring the boss, then, bureaucrats feel they ought to resist the initiatives of the short-term amateurs the Chief sends to represent him and that they can get away with it. So they do.

The Means of Presidential Influence

At first glance it seems as if the President ought to be a better match for the bureaucracy. Every January we hear about the President's budget. We hear about his legislative program and how his Cabinet is going to bring management efficiency, ideological zeal, or the unlikely combination of both, to the running of government. Each of the last half-dozen Presidents has told us that the federal government needed a thorough-going organizational shake-up and that he was the man to do it. We all know that bureaucrats are frightened of government reorganization, are subject to the legal authority of a layer of political executives, need legal authorization to do much of anything, and couldn't function at all without dollars. So how come the politician part of the bureaucrat isn't really afraid of the Chief?

Personnel Selection

Let's start with the President's team. The President has the opportunity to nominate approximately 2,500 men and women for key policy-making positions in the federal bureaucracy. Cabinet and sub-Cabinet officers, regulatory commission members, and even certain agency heads or bureau chiefs attained their current positions in part because the President or someone close to him felt they were "right" for the job. They remember that, of course, just as they remember that should they suddenly change from "right" to "wrong" the job could be gone.

Loyalty to the man, whether born of personal ties, ideological commitment, or just plain gratitude, is a powerful motivator. So is job protection. These 2,500 men and women are, in a very real sense, the President's team. Still, they do not succeed in putting the President's stamp on most of what goes on in the executive branch. The reasons are two. First of all, they can't. They lack the resources to do it. Second, they do not try as hard as we might expect. Loyal as these men and women may be to the President, it is not their only loyalty.

There is ample reason to conclude that the President's team faces an uphill struggle when attempting to influence the actions of the agencies nominally under his supervision. Cabinet and sub-Cabinet officials also lack the time, knowledge, and interest for effective supervision of their respective organizational domains. To be sure, none of these individuals finds himself or herself facing the immense pressures that face the Chief Executive, but their situation is analogous. There is too much to know, too much to do, and too little time in which to do it. Further, they face a career staff wary of allowing too much influence over a department's constituent agencies, and frequently possessed of sufficient statutory authority and political support to fend off secretarial efforts at control.[11]

The extent to which a Cabinet member and his or her deputies can control a department undoubtedly varies from one department to another. Controlling the Defense Department in the face of its size, complexity, and the independent political power of the uniformed services is surely a more difficult task than managing the Department of Labor, but neither is going to be easy. Indeed, with minor qualifications and/or reservations, I suspect most of the men and women who have served in Cabinet and sub-Cabinet positions in the past twenty years would agree with Harold Seidman that "a department head's job is akin to that of a major university president and subject to the same frustrations. His principal duties involve matters which are unrelated to the internal administration and management of the institution. So far as his subordinates are concerned, he is the institution's ceremonial head, chief fund raiser, and protector of institutional values and territory. An informal check reveals that a department head may spend 25 percent or more of his time in meetings with members of the Congress and appearances before congressional committees, and probably an equivalent amount of time in public relations work such as speech making and cultivating agency constituencies. Another block of time is devoted to White House conferences and meetings of interagency and advisory committees. Minimal time is left for managing the department, even if a secretary is one of the rare political executives with a taste for administration." [12]

Though they can accomplish far less than they and their President might like, these top-level executives are not powerless. But, even when they can and do have an effect on agency policy making, that effect is not always an automatic extension of presidential priorities. These men and women are loyal to the President, but they are also loyal to the bureaus and agencies that make up their departments and to the constituencies associated with them. This second loyalty, uncomfortable as it may sometimes become, stems from two sources.

First, a Cabinet or sub-Cabinet official who alienates the career staff of his or her department's constituent bureaus can accomplish little if anything. No large organization can be run by command, particularly if subordinates have considerable knowledge and power of their own. This, of course, is the situation in which most political executives find themselves. To secure the cooperation, or at least the neutrality, of these agencies, a Secretary and his or her deputies must offer something in return, and, often as not, that something is to plead the agencies' cases before the President. To paraphrase former NASA chief James Webb, the political executive is the man in the middle, and he has to remain on good terms with both sides. [13]

Second, presidential patterns of appointment to these Cabinet and sub-Cabinet positions virtually guarantee that the men and women chosen to carry the President's policies into the bureaucracy will be sympathetic to the various constellations of bureaus, agencies, and clientele groups that make up their respective departments. Secretaries of Agriculture are nearly always Midwesterners with long-standing ties to the Department's constituencies. Clifford Hardin and Earl Butz came from major land grant colleges (Nebraska and Purdue, respectively) and each had served his school as Agriculture Dean. Robert Bergland, Jimmy Carter's choice for the job, was a U.S. Representative from Minnesota and a member of the House Agriculture Committee, while Mr. Reagan's first selection for the post, John Block, was Agriculture Secretary for the state of Illinois.[14] Illinois, not coincidentally, is the state with the largest chapter of the American Farm Bureau Federation, the farm producer group with the oldest and closest ties to the Agriculture Department.[15] When Richard Lyng, a Californian with lifelong ties to agriculture became Secretary in early 1986, the DOA's second in command, another Californian, resigned. The reason cited: too much California. The Interior Department is as much a Western preserve at the top as it is at the bottom with the likes of Stewart Udall (Arizona), Walter Hickel (Alaska), Cecil Andrus (Idaho), James Watt (Wyoming via Colorado), and Donald Hodel (Oregon) occupying the Secretary's chair.[16] The patterns are somewhat less clear cut at departments like Treasury, Labor, and Commerce, but patterns do exist, nonetheless.[17]

When we move to the sub-Cabinet level, the connection to a department's constituent bureaus and clientele groups becomes even more apparent. Some recent examples include: John F. Lehman, Jr., president of a Washington, D.C., defense consulting firm as Secretary of the Navy; Ray Barnhart, Texas Highway Commissioner, as administrator of the Federal Highway Administration; Donald P. Hodel, Oregon attorney, energy consultant and former chief of the Bonneville Power Administration as Under Secretary of the Interior (then on to Energy Secretary and finally back to the top job at Interior); Donald T. Hovde, former president of the National Association of Realtors, as Under Secretary of Housing and Urban Development; Richard E. Lyng, former president of the American Meat Institute, as Under Secretary, then Secretary, of Agriculture; C. W. McMillan, vice-president for government affairs of the National Cattleman's Association as Assistant Secretary of Agriculture; and, Joseph F.

Wright, Jr., an executive of Citicorp, as Deputy Secretary of Commerce.[18]

Presidents adhere to these patterns for both personal and political reasons. The personal reasons are two. Presidents, like members of the Congress and career bureaucrats, believe that the groups involved and concerned with a particular department deserve some special consideration from that department, and representation at the top is one way to grant it to them. In addition to this concern for the department's constituencies, Presidents want to find men and women for these positions who have at least a working knowledge of the policies, programs, and organizations they will be called upon to oversee. It makes sense to go to the clientele groups or others in the appropriate issue network to find such expertise. A man who has run one of the largest state highway departments in the country should be able to step into the Federal Highway Administration with some idea of what is going on. Similarly, a man with experience as the chief economist for the Senate Agriculture Committee should be prepared for the job of chief economist at the Department of Agriculture.[19] These appointment patterns simply seem logical to a President.

As much philosophical and technological sense as these appointment patterns make to a President, they make even better political sense. The vast majority of Americans would be hard pressed to supply the names of ten of the 2,500 people the President has appointed to these key bureaucratic positions. One doubts that more than a fraction of the citizenry knows of the existence of the post Assistant Secretary of Agriculture for Marketing and Transportation Services, let alone that on January 29, 1981, Ronald Reagan selected C. W. McMillan, vice-president for government affairs of the National Cattleman's Association, to exercise that particular public trust.[20] Someone must have been happy with the choice. Mr. McMillan was easily confirmed within sixty days of his nomination.[21]

To put it more directly, Presidents are well aware that except for a handful of highly visible posts like State and Defense, their appointments to the bureaucracy will attract little attention from the general public. But the man in the White House is equally aware that every one of these appointments is important to the clientele groups of the various departments and their constituent agencies. A President stands to gain, or to lose, support among these groups based on his appointment decisions. Since the President knows the importance of such groups to his political health, as well as the importance of these nominations to the clientele groups and their evaluation of him, it should come as no surprise that Presidents choose to make Cabinet, and especially sub-Cabinet, appointments that will be popular with the groups served or regulated by a particular department or agency. They lose nothing with the general public and may gain a great deal with important organized interest groups.

Presidents are also painfully aware that these are nominations —that is, that the men and women selected for these positions must pass the test of Senate confirmation. In all but the rarest of cases, the major Senate hurdle is found at the committee level. At the sub-Cabinet level, particularly, committee approval is tantamount to Senate approval. Senate committees, like their House counterparts, have close ties with the organized interest groups concerned with their area of policy.[22] Consequently, the Senators who will have the greatest say on Agriculture Department appointments are those on the Agriculture Committee, and they are men and women from agricultural states with close personal and political ties to agriculture producers and the groups that represent them.[23] Objections to a particular nominee from those producer groups would be given considerable weight when the committee considered the fate of that individual. Presidents know that, and would prefer not to suffer, or even to risk, the embarrassment of having a nominee rejected. The easiest way to avoid that sort of embarrassment is to send the Senate the names of people acceptable to those clientele groups. It is not uncommon for Presidents to seek to guarantee the acceptability of their nominees by prior consultation with representatives of clientele groups, members of the Senate committees, or both.

The impact of these appointment patterns, of course, is a set

of political executives with dual loyalties. With some past connection to the Chief Executive or someone close to him, and
serving at his pleasure, they are loyal to the man and his policies.
The pull of past ties, and the expectation of future association
with the bureaus, agencies, and clientele groups that are part of
their departments makes them loyal to these constituencies, and
for a growing number there is the added tie of shared expertise
gained by virtue of a long commitment to this set of issues, programs, and policies. Like anyone else called upon to serve two
masters, these political executives are placed in an uncomfortable
position. Standing in the middle one can be run over from either
side. But that is the nature of the job, so they will try to balance
these conflicting demands and, in the process, be less than complete representatives of the President and his preferences.

After reading the past several pages you may be beginning to
think that the Chief might as well select his team of political
executives by making random choices from the membership list
of the Washington, D.C., Bar Association or *Who's Who in the
Midwest*. Not so. A determined President who believes that a
particular agency is too vigorous in pursuing its policy objectives can use his appointment powers to frustrate that agency
and its people. Examples of this kind of presidential success are
easy enough to find.

In 1971, Richard Nixon decided something had to be done to
slow the growth in the nation's welfare rolls. So he eased out his
old friend Bob Finch—then Secretary of Health, Education, and
Welfare—and Finch's chief welfare lieutenant, John Venneman.
Their replacements were Caspar Weinberger and James Dwight,
fresh from their stints as point men for Ronald Reagan's attack
on the California welfare system. Known respectively as "Cap
the Knife" and "Atilla the Hun," Weinberger and Dwight left
key management positions vacant, created new staff positions—
in some cases entire staff units—and generally demoralized the
federal government's welfare careerists. The most devastating
blow came when the two men issued a "quality control directive"

aimed at eliminating eligibility determination mistakes by state and local welfare officials.

A caseworker can, and given the incredible complexity of the welfare system almost inevitably will, say Yes to some applicants who should have been turned away and deny benefits to some he or she should have declared eligible. Further, it is possible to miscalculate the size of the grant to which a particular applicant is entitled. Weinberger and Dwight declared that saying Yes when the answer was No and paying too much were errors we could no longer abide—the opposite two mistakes were OK, however—and proposed funds cutoffs if a state's eligibility error rate was greater than 3 percent or if its overpayments exceeded 5 percent of its total dollar grants. To no one's surprise, all of the close calls began to go against the welfare applicants and Nixon, Weinberger, and Dwight could claim a victory.[24]

Just for the record, federal courts subsequently concluded that the decision had been reached in a manner that was "arbitrary and capricious" and ordered it re-evaluated. The departure of all of the principals dampened enthusiasm for an appeal and things drifted back toward normal. Still, welfare rolls held close to steady from the time the rule was imposed until the Carter Administration took over, so one can hardly call the effect inconsequential.[25]

Ronald Reagan has used top-level appointments as a weapon against career bureaucrats just as successfully and a lot more frequently than did Mr. Nixon. Probably his best-known effort came at the Environmental Protection Agency in the early days of his administration. Anne Gorsuch, soon to become Burford, was something of a surprise selection as EPA Administrator. Named —along with her future husband, William Burford, whom Mr. Reagan selected to head the Bureau of Land Management—by the Sierra Club as one of Colorado's "Dirty Half-Dozen," her environmental record made even the relatively conservative National Wildlife Federation uneasy. Eventually she was brought down by a combination of style and her conflict with Congress over whether or not some agency documents should be delivered to the members of the relevant House and Senate committees, but in the interim she created an organizational climate like EPA had never known. With vacancies unfilled and direct pressure on regional directors and staff to go easier on polluting industries, it became a nightmare for career staff used to the likes of Russell Train and William Ruckelshaus. Nowhere were the policy consequences better illustrated than in the managerial bungling and political maneuvering that characterized the handling of EPA's so-called Superfund.

Later on in his administration, Mr. Reagan discovered one of Richard Nixon's favorite tricks, the acting administrator. An acting bureau chief, agency director, or assistant secretary doesn't have to pass muster with the Senate. He or she can wreak a good bit of havoc on behalf of the Chief and then head on home without so much as a single subcommittee vote on his or her qualifications.

On Monday, March 31, 1986, Charles L. Heatherly took over as Acting Administrator of the Small Business Administration. Mr. Reagan had tried to kill the SBA a couple of times before, but Congress just wouldn't let him do it. Enter Mr. Heatherly. On April 1, the Acting Administrator fired five of the SBA's ten regional administrators and nailed a sixth—who had been out of town on the first—the following day. Within two weeks, the flak from Senators and small business lobbyists was thick, but Weatherly, presumably with his Chief still behind him, was terrorizing the SBA and all of its supporters. An agency badly weakened by budget cuts was now in worse shape than ever.

Terry Moe's study of the National Labor Relations Board provides a clear and balanced overview of the problems and prospects that confront a President as he uses his appointment powers to attempt to influence bureaucratic policy making. The best way to pull together what I have said in this section of the chapter is to tell you what he found.

The NLRB hears complaints of unfair labor practices. Management can complain about unions, unions about management.

No President could possibly be unaware of the partisan, and ultimately personal, fallout that is almost certain to accompany the Board's decisions in these emotionally charged labor disputes. Moe found that Presidents know precisely who cares about these decisions and why, and every Chief Executive from Ike on has tried to use his appointments, especially the crucial designation of Chairman, to keep the Board on his side. It has worked, and, as Professor Moe points out, the impact has always been particularly noticeable when a new President assumed office. Eisenhower inherited a pro-labor Board and turned it around, Jack Kennedy and Lyndon Johnson turned it back, and the beat went on through the sixties and seventies. These appointments mattered all right, but Professor Moe found three pretty good reasons why these Presidents couldn't use them to gain effective control over NLRB decision making.

First, these, like all other appointments, don't always turn out the way the President plans them. One of Dwight Eisenhower's appointees—a man named John H. Fanning—turned out to be far more liberal and pro-labor than anyone had guessed. He also stayed a long time, finally being named Chairman by Jimmy Carter in 1977.

Next come the inevitable complications imposed by the politics of the appointment process. In late 1971 and early 1972, Richard Nixon had the chance to make two appointments and tip the existing pro-labor balance on the Board. But he wanted some labor union support in his re-election bid and reappointment of the liberal Fanning was part of the price. The other seat that would have become vacant belonged to a Black Republican who wanted to stay. He, too, was reappointed. Three years later, Gerald Ford by-passed the opportunity to put a hard-nosed conservative on the Board when he opted instead to appoint its first woman member.

Finally, when Board attitudes shift it sets off a very interesting chain reaction. At first the staff responds to the new direction by calling more of the close ones in the direction the Board seems to be headed. Word filters down and whichever side now has the advantage begins to file more, and, according to Moe, more questionable, complaints. Eventually the staff and the Board itself begin to move the pendulum back and await another swing.[26]

So, if the job doesn't belong by tradition to some organized interest group, and doesn't have to be used as part of a political trade-off, and doesn't offer the perfect opportunity for a symbolic appointment, and if the person appointed acts the way the President and his advisors expected him or her to act, the Chief is on his way. There will be the inevitable attempt at cooptation by the career staff, but that doesn't always work. EPA careerists never owned so much as a small slice of Anne Burford. Agency and departmental traditions, subject matter complexity, and time pressures will add in more frustrations, but some of the President's team will overcome even these. There are all kinds of constraints on the use of the appointment power as a tool for influencing bureaucratic policy making. But it does work, and for a President who wants to slow/stop/frustrate bureaucracy, it can work fairly well.

Legislation

The law matters a great deal to bureaucrats. It sets the goals toward which agencies are expected to work and provides some indication, however vague, of the means to be used to get there. The law also puts limits on bureaucrats. Any agency that engages in actions for which it lacks statutory authority is a better than even money bet to find itself in court explaining why. In fact, an agency that doesn't do something it is empowered to do may well find itself hauled before a judge to explain why it didn't do it. But laws can also open up opportunities. There had long been a good deal of professional concern with questions of workplace dangers in both the Department of Labor and HEW, but serious action had to wait for the Occupational Safety and Health Act of 1970.[27] Likewise, Bureau of Mines safety inspectors were hardly able to protect American coal miners when the only two enforcement powers open to them were to "publicize" the violations or close down the mine.[28]

Spelling out goals, setting limits, and providing opportunities, shaping the law can be a very effective mechanism for controlling bureaucracy. The question is, can the President use it? The answer: For the Chief, it is the best of tools, it is the worst of tools.

If an agency wishes to embark upon a course of action for which it lacks statutory authority, and the President wants to prevent that, his hand will be difficult to beat. His cards—the veto and the process known as central or legislative clearance—are pretty easy for him to play and almost certain to bring him a victory.

The operation of the legislative clearance process is fairly simple and quite effective.[29] Any agency with a proposal for legislation must submit that proposal to the Legislative Reference Division of the Office of Management and Budget. The Legislative Reference Division staff, which consists of career OMB officials, then reviews the legislation to determine if it is consistent with the President's policy goals and preferences. If the staff is convinced that the legislation is consistent with White House preferences, the agency is given the go ahead to have it introduced into the Congress. If it is convinced that the proposal is not in line with presidential policy directions, Legislative Reference informs the agency of that determination and the proposal is supposed to be dropped. At this point the disgruntled agency can appeal the OMB decision to the White House, and, if turned down again, could presumably go around the President to a receptive member of Congress and get the legislation introduced anyway. This "end run" strategy is dangerous, of course, since it will undoubtedly anger the Legislative Reference Division, and quite likely incur presidential wrath as well. Hard data on the frequency of agency end runs is almost impossible to come by since agency officials and friendly members of Congress tend to deny such conspiracies, but Stephen Wayne has concluded that they are quite infrequent.[30] Finally, in those cases in which there is some question either about what the President's preferences really are or about whether or not a particular bill is consistent with those preferences, the Legislative Reference staff will consult with OMB's top leadership or, if need be, with the White House staff or the President himself.

Beginning with John Kennedy, every Chief Executive has insisted on greater and greater White House involvement in the central clearance process. As a result, this screening of bureaucratic requests for new authority really is carried out with a presidential eye and in the process prevents most agencies from getting very far when they seek the authority to pursue policies the President finds inappropriate.

Should an agency sneak past central clearance, there is always the veto. It is a bit riskier—vetoes make headlines, as well as some enemies, and Congress can override them—but the odds still favor the President.

The Chief can even use this substantial blocking authority as a bargaining chip. He can easily say to an agency head, "I don't particularly care if you get the authority to do that or not, but I'll see to it that you don't unless you start (stop) doing ——." The threat won't automatically work, but if the agency really does want (need) that new authority it must at least seriously consider responding to the President's request.

At the opposite end of the spectrum is the agency currently pursuing policies it has pursued for years under authority it has had for as long as anyone can remember. A President who finds himself annoyed by these policies is going to find it very nearly impossible to get them changed. For here the power of the President really is the "power to persuade,"[31] and he is dealing with people who won't find him all that persuasive, on this issue anyway.

For all of the reasons discussed earlier in this chapter, the bureaucrats involved will not be particularly impressed by the President's claim that he has a better idea. They are the experts, not he. His people are little better. The policy is tried and true and this President might change his mind, or even be gone, by the time the consequences of the change are known. The Chief could turn his attention to the Congress; that is, he could attempt to convince the legislative branch to withdraw the authority to pursue this particular course of action. For reasons explored in the next chapter, this is not likely to work either. He must begin at the committee or subcommittee level and here he will face other self-styled experts with an intellectual and political commitment to those policies very similar to that of the agency staff.

This is not to say the President can never win in these situations. If an agency has a vital legislative initiative pending it becomes susceptible to White House pressure and it may compromise. Still, in most cases, if an agency already has the authority and is using it, the President has a pretty slim chance of getting that agency to change its mind.

In between those circumstances in which the President is almost certain to win and those in which he is nearly certain to lose, are some in which even Jimmy the Greek would be hard pressed to determine the odds on the Chief's success. If, for example, an agency clearly has the authority to engage in a certain set of actions, but has never done so, a President's chances for success should be better. It is usually easier to persuade someone not to do something in the first place than to persuade him or her to stop doing it later. There is a lot less face saving to be done.

Or consider the many cases in which agency authority is ambiguous. Suppose an agency wishes to embark upon a course of action but is not certain that its legislative mandate permits it to do so. The Attorney General is the one empowered to interpret the meaning of statutes and that gives the President another opportunity to say No. An Attorney General's interpretation can be overturned by Congress or the courts, but that takes a good deal of agency time and effort, and should an initial court test go against the agency, only the Solicitor General can authorize an appeal of the court's ruling.[32] Indeed, any time an agency loses in court, only the Justice Department can OK further legal action by that agency. These Justice Department powers are not insurmountable obstacles, but, where agency authority is unclear, they do offer the President one more small string to pull in his effort to manipulate bureaucracy.

Finally, the President may have positive goals; that is, he may want an agency to start doing something. Whenever the Chief wants to start something, he must persuade, so he is automatically toward the weak end of the continuum, though just how far toward that end will depend upon who he must persuade and how great the distance between the agency's current policy and the President's alternative.

This is as good a place as any to complicate matters even further. I have been talking about the President's ability to use the legislative powers of his office to influence bureaucracy as if all Presidents were created equal. Far from it. Presidents themselves vary in persuasive abilities, and even if they did not, the political health of a particular Chief Executive at a particular moment is always a key ingredient in any President's success at convincing people to do it his way. The statement, "The President is solidly behind this!" carried a lot of weight in Washington in the summer of 1964. It wasn't worth much a decade later, but had made a comeback by 1984. As if that is not enough, there is also the question of who in the Congress is interested in this particular issue and where he or she stands. Catching a lot of us off guard, Richard Nixon backed a major reform of the nation's welfare system in 1969 only to run smack into Russell Long and an embarrassing defeat.[33]

The list of complicating factors could be extended and firm generalizations about the President's ability to use legislation as a weapon in his struggle with bureaucracy are hard to come by. Still, I believe it is possible to say that when an agency wants to do something the President opposes, if that agency lacks the authority to do it, the Chief has an excellent chance of getting his way. In any other set of circumstances, we are talking about degrees of weakness. The President will win some and he will lose some, and he will win some kinds oftener than others, but outside of that one important situation—an agency that needs his OK for new initiatives—the long-run odds clearly favor the bureaucrats and their supporters.

Structure

Questions of bureaucratic structure—that is, questions of the creation, abolition, or reorganization of government agencies—as well as the assignment of programs to agencies, agencies to departments, and statutory authority to specific officials, are generally considered deadly dull and frequently thought to be insignificant. Dull they may be. Insignificant they are not. The policy consequences that flow from the answers to three of these structural questions are enormous and a President who could influence those answers could have a significant impact on bureaucratic policy making.

Start with the question of the placement of legal authority. Which government official shall possess the legal right to commit the United States government to a particular course of action? Who will be empowered to sign a lease to drill for oil in the Santa Barbara Channel, mine coal on public land in Utah, or cut timber in the Kaniksu National Forest of eastern Washington?

Such authority could be vested in the President, but it rarely is. The normal choices are Cabinet Secretaries, agency heads, or even program administrators. Each of these operates at a very different level of the executive branch and, more to the point, from a very different perspective. Specifically, program administrators are generally narrow but dedicated specialists committed to a particular view of sound policy, Cabinet Secretaries are men and women caught between loyalty to the President and concern for their departments, and agency heads are somewhere in between depending, among other things, on how much say this Chief had in their selection and their own current political standing.

From the President's viewpoint, placing legal authority in the hands of Cabinet Secretaries gives him a far greater chance for influence than would the placement of that authority in the hands of agency heads or, worst of all presidential worlds, career program administrators. Even Ronald Reagan might have found James Watt's offshore oil development plan a bit ambitious, but he surely preferred it to the sort of plan likely to be produced by the Interior Department careerists and, in any event, he could always get rid of Mr. Watt, or any other Secretary, should the need arise.

A second crucial structural question revolves around the assignment of specific programs to specific agencies. Because agencies differ so much in attitude and outlook they will also differ in how they would administer a particular program. For over half a century, enforcement of mine safety legislation belonged to the Bureau of Mines. Committed to its primary goal of "ensur[ing] that the Nation has adequate mineral supplies for security and other needs"[34] and hamstrung by the lack of effective enforcement tools, the Bureau did little. In fact, for a time, Bureau safety inspections were conducted with advance notice of several weeks, allowing owners to engage in all sorts of temporary safety measures. When the 1977 Mine Safety Act moved responsibility for safety inspection to the newly created Mine Safety and Health Administration located in the Department of Labor, everything changed. Within a year, MSHA was conducting safety inspections without search warrants, let alone advance notice, and fighting for the legal right to conduct such warrantless inspections when the practice was challenged.[35] The agency won, and until Reagan appointees in the Labor Department managed to slow its zeal, such inspections were common and the imposition of penalties vigorous.[36]

If a President is unhappy with the operation of a particular program, he can look for an agency likely to implement that program in a way more to his liking. If he finds such an agency and can move the program from its present home to what he sees as a more congenial spot, the President will clearly have made his presence felt in bureaucracy.

Finally, there are the ever-present questions of creating new agencies or abolishing old ones, merging bureaus, regrouping them within departments, or even moving them from one department to another. As Harold Seidman notes, this sort of tinkering "has become almost a religion in Washington."[37] It is hard to remember a single administration that hasn't made some noise about the need to reorganize the federal bureaucracy as a means of achieving the twin gods of economy and efficiency. Seidman is clearly correct when he says that proponents of reorganization have vastly overstated its potential impact on public policy, but that is not to say that abolishing a bureau and spreading its functions around, moving an agency from one department to another, or creating a new organization to handle a set of previously scattered responsibilities would affect nothing.

Despite the general pattern of agency independence that characterizes the executive branch, agencies do have to accommodate their departmental superiors to one degree or another and trading one set for another, along with trading one entire departmental history, tradition, and mission for another, is bound to have some effect. The Mine Safety and Health Administration simply could not be as aggressive a proponent of safety if it were moved from Labor to Interior. On the other hand, the Office of Surface Mining Reclamation and Enforcement might find some new teeth were it to leave Interior for the Environmental Protection Agency. Likewise, the decision to create EPA and "centralize" the implementation of certain important environmental goals made a difference in both the speed and the consistency of our air and water clean-up. Were we to abolish OSHA and spread its functions to existing units in several departments or merge the Office of Surface Mining Reclamation and Enforcement with the Bureau of Mines we would almost surely get less vigorous enforcement of occupational safety and strip mining laws respectively.

Presidents know these things matter, and, consequently, that if they can play a major role in these reorganization decisions they can exercise some control over bureaucracy. They know all right, but their influence over the formal structure of the executive branch is so limited that the knowledge does them little good.

In the first place, despite the fact that nearly all Presidents pay lip service to the need for and importance of restructuring the federal bureaucracy, seldom do they follow through on the rhetoric. Jimmy Carter told the Democratic Platform Committee, "We must give top priority to a drastic and thorough reorganization of the Federal bureaucracy." [38] He still ended up scuttling most of the comprehensive plans developed by his Reorganization Project. [39] On a similar note, Richard Nixon claimed that the primary cause of governmental ineffectiveness was "a matter of machinery," [40] and proposed a sweeping reorganization of the entire executive branch. Yet, as Harold Seidman reports, "on the very day that the Under-Secretary of Agriculture J. Phil Campbell was dutifully testifying before the House Committee that the Department of Agriculture ought to be abolished as a constituency and clientele-oriented department, the president, disturbed by the political repercussions of declining farm prices, announced that the plan had been abandoned and that the Department of Agriculture would be retained as the spokesman for farmers." [41]

Even if a Chief Executive is willing to devote his time, energy, and prestige to restructuring efforts, he must still confront a wary, sometimes even hostile Congress. Whether he wants to shift a program from one agency to another, create one agency out of two, or just require the Department Secretary's signature where an agency head's used to do, the Congress will have its say.

Programs are moved and authority assigned by law, so the President's problems and prospects have, in effect, already been discussed in the previous section. He can usually stop Congress from doing what he doesn't want, but when it comes to getting the legislative branch to move programs or shift authority from the agency to the department level, the story is very different. The normal congressional reaction to any such White House-backed proposal was effectively summarized by former HEW

Secretary John Gardner in an appearance before the Senate
Government Operations Committee:

"Some elements in Congress and some special interest lobbies
have never really wanted the departmental Secretaries to be
strong. As everyone in this room knows but few people outside
of Washington understand, questions of public policy nominally
lodged with the Secretary are often decided far beyond the Secretary's reach by a trinity—not exactly a holy trinity—consisting
of (1) representatives of an outside lobby, (2) middle-level bureaucrats, and (3) selected members of Congress. . . .

Participants in such durable alliances do not want the departmental Secretaries strengthened. And they oppose even more
vigorously *any reorganization that might shake up the alliance.*
If the subject matter is shifted to another congressional committee, the congressional leg of the trinity may be broken. If the
departments are reorganized, a stranger may appear on the bureaucratic leg of the triangle. The outside special interests are
particularly resistant to such change. It took them years to dig
their particular tunnel into the public vault, and they don't want
the vault moved." [42]

When it comes to reorganization (creation/abolition/merger
etc.) the President has two options. He can propose positive legislation, as Jimmy Carter did in the creation of the Departments of
Education and Energy, or as Harry Truman did with DOD or
Lyndon Johnson with the Department of Transportation. Here,
again, he faces all of the problems of convincing Congress to go
along. If he wishes to avoid the problems inherent in this approach, the Chief can submit a reorganization plan. That is, he
can if he has been granted the authority to do so. It is a long
story, but important enough that a shortened version of it needs
to be told.

Just short of fifty years ago, the Roosevelt Administration asked
Congress for the right to do a little tinkering with executive
branch machinery. After a long battle and a host of weakening
amendments, the President got the authority to submit specific

reorganization plans.[43] If Congress failed to disapprove, the plan had the force of law. Some significant reorganization has been accomplished under this authority including Dwight Eisenhower's creation of HEW, Nixon's start of both EPA and the Drug Enforcement Administration, and Lyndon Johnson's reorganization of the government of the District of Columbia.[44]

Unfortunately, from the President's perspective anyway, there are two rather large impediments to the effective use of presidential reorganization plans as a means of restructuring the federal bureaucracy. The authority to issue such plans can be withdrawn by Congress and each new extension of that authority in the last three decades has brought more restrictions on its use.

Presidential reorganization authority is granted by statute and it is traditional to require periodic reauthorization, that is, to say precisely when such authority will expire. Three times in the past twenty years—in a fit of pique over John Kennedy's efforts to use it to create a Department of Housing and Urban Affairs, as a reaction to Watergate, and most recently as part of a puzzled response to the Supreme Court decision to strike down the legislative veto[45]—Congress has let this authority lapse. Any President must be cautious in using powers he knows Congress can and has pulled out from under his predecessors.

Even more significant have been the substantive restrictions Congress has placed on the President's use of his reorganization authority. As early as 1949 the law provided for a one house legislative veto, and subsequent extensions of the authority have added the prohibition against the creation of Cabinet departments and, perhaps most important of all, a provision preventing the President from proposing the elimination of any agency or program created by statute.[46] In short, before the Supreme Court ruling and the subsequent congressional decision to let the authority lapse, the President could do pretty much what Congress would let him do and, as often as not, that wasn't very much.

Reorganization is probably the least effective weapon in the President's arsenal, but it can work if he and his team are determined enough to make it work. Richard Nixon, Caspar Weinberger, and James Dwight were that determined.

The Johnson Administration had attempted to centralize responsibility for the federal government's expanding role in the nation's welfare system by creating the Social and Rehabilitation Service and by assigning responsibility for all of the categorical assistance programs (Aid to Families with Dependent Children, Aid to the Blind, Aid to the Permanently and Totally Disabled, and Old Age Assistance) to one of its constituent units, the Assistance Payments Administration. Even before Weinberger and Dwight launched their all-out attack, the Nixon Administration had begun chipping away at the power of APA. First the Nixon people got Congress to accept the creation of a unit called the Community Services Administration that would absorb the social services functions from APA. At this point Mr. Nixon was still flirting with his Family Assistance Plan and it was his intention to have that program administered by the Social Security Administration, not the welfare people. So the specialists at APA or other SRS units were frozen out of the planning process completely. Lots of people left both units and they weren't replaced. When FAP failed in Congress and Nixon brought in Weinberger and Dwight, they transferred all quality control and evaluation functions from APA to the newly created Office of Management attached directly to the office of James Dwight, head of SRS. It was this unit that launched the drive to purge the rolls of ineligibles described earlier in this chapter. The dismantling of APA and the near destruction of SRS was pretty much completed in January 1974, when all of the adult assistance categories were folded together into the Supplemental Security Income program assigned to the Social Security Administration. SRS received its formal burial in 1977.[47]

These various structural maneuvers were an important ingredient in the Nixon-Weinberger-Dwight attack on the nation's welfare system. They played an integral part in the success of that attack, by isolating the welfare specialists and freezing them out of the decision-making process. The resulting lowered morale and frustration drove people away, weakening these organizational units even further until they reached a point at which they were too drained to fight, even for their very existence. In the meantime, welfare policy was being made elsewhere by people far more to Mr. Nixon's liking. It is true that Congress had to play the role of silent partner in some of this—that is, had to "fail to disapprove"—and it did. It may be that Congress didn't mind what was happening, or it may be that these seemingly minor changes paled by comparison with Mr. Nixon's massive restructuring proposal that had Congress buzzing for a large part of 1971.[48] Whatever the cause, Congress acquiesced when it had to and Mr. Nixon pushed welfare specialists aside and welfare policy where he wanted it to go.

Even if a President loses a particular reorganization battle, he may get some of what he wants in terms of policy consequences. Reorganization fights can be exhausting. And bloody. While an agency is fighting one it is going to be using up a lot of time and energy and depleting its reserve of political capital. It may well be forced to slow down a lot of its substantive activities just to continue the fight. If that was what the President was after, he got some of it, even if the scoreboard says he lost.

Structure affects policy and the President can affect structure, but not often and not systematically. Some of the limitations on his power are self-imposed—a lack of real effort by the Chief—but it is very easy to see why a President, short on time and hoping to make some sort of mark on a particular public policy, would use his own supply of political capital to go after that policy directly rather than trying to accomplish the same result through the round-about method of reorganization. Besides, the Congress is reluctant to allow much tinkering with the executive branch structure anyway, a limitation far more important than any the President imposes on himself and one more good reason why the Chief is likely to look elsewhere for the tools to control bureaucracy.

The Budget

Agencies need money. If it is to protect American miners, the Mine Safety and Health Administration has to inspect the mines in which they work. Inspectors have to travel to the mines, their reports have to be typed, copied, and filed, and they expect to be paid. Fewer MSHA dollars would surely mean fewer inspectors, fewer inspectors fewer inspections and, in all probability, fewer complaints against the mine owners. This is precisely what happened in 1981 and 1982, when MSHA found its budget reduced.[49] The same could happen to OSHA, it could happen to the EPA, it could even happen to the Department of Agriculture. If and when it does, policy consequences are inevitable.

But what role does the President play in all of this? Can he have a significant impact on the number of dollars the U.S. government devotes to inspecting mines, researching the effects of acid rain, or supporting the price of soybeans? And whether or not he can, how often does he make the effort?

From the beginnings of the executive budget process up through the end of the 1960's, the answers were No and Seldom. The budgets sent by the Presidents of that half century were executive branch documents, in a very real sense the sum of their parts. As Aaron Wildavsky pointed out in 1964, the budget was put together in pieces, and in stages, with each of the key participants playing clearly defined and mutually agreed-upon roles, operating in a context of shared norms, and secure in the knowledge that they would all have another chance next year if anything went drastically wrong.[50] Agencies were program advocates, Department Secretaries tried to balance loyalty to the President against their role as "chief fund raiser,"[51] and OMB (BOB) examiners did a detailed review based on their own professional judgments, most concluding that they were "doing the right thing by pursuing policies in the public interest . . . [and convincing] themselves that the President would support them if only he had the time and inclination to go into the matter as deeply as they had." [52] All of these executive branch participants kept a watchful eye on the relevant House and Senate Appropriations Subcommittees and the whole process ground on with little if any presidential influence. To be sure, a President could attempt to muscle in on the act through his people at OMB, or personally just before the document was to be signed, but the budget was so big, so complex, and so dull that few ever did it, and when they did, the intervention was clearly an isolated instance that came as a surprise to all concerned. Probably more typical for Presidents of this era was the Eisenhower reaction to "his" fiscal 1958 budget. Ike expressed dismay and no small amount of annoyance at the size of the budget, much as if he had played no role in its preparation and didn't know how it could have happened.[53] The Presidents probably all felt that way, but only Ike said it publicly, the day "his" budget was submitted to the Congress.

But times have changed.[54] Old norms are breaking down or gone altogether, old roles abandoned, money can be spent in a variety of ways outside of the traditional appropriations process, and in no serious sense is the budget document the President submits a real plan for, or record of, the taxing and spending decisions of the national government for the year that appears on its cover. In this new, and immensely confusing, setting what has happened to the President's ability to influence policy through dollars?

If you pay a great deal of attention to the headlines of the 1980's, you would just about have to conclude that Ronald Reagan figured out how to use the budgetary sword to cow almost the entire herd of bureaucratic dragons. Allowing for a good bit of exaggeration by everyone involved, it still appears that this particular President has played a significant role in reducing the amount of money that most agencies have to spend. Though the resulting policy consequences may not always be as severe as bureaucratic defenders try to paint them, they have been real. The Mine Safety and Health Administration first felt the presidential knife in the last year of the Carter Administration, but

Mr. Reagan accelerated the cuts. The result was fewer inspectors, fewer inspections, fewer citations, and, ultimately, the highest death toll in the coal mines in a decade.[55] Coal mines are dangerous places. We might have had an increase in fatalities even without these budget cuts and I certainly don't want to imply that either Jimmy Carter or Ronald Reagan was indifferent to the fate of the men and women who mine the nation's coal. The point is simply that budgets do affect policy, sometimes in dramatic and not very pleasant ways.

Mr. Reagan had a real impact on a series of budgets all right, and there is no doubt that, outside of the Defense Department, the effect has been to force bureaucracy to do less than it used to do and less than it wants to do. The way in which he did it, however, is not likely to be open to his successors, for his greatest impact on the budgets of his first six years came on the revenue side and occurred before anyone really knew what was happening.

It may be hard to recall after six straight years of budgetary wrangling, but Mr. Reagan's original proposal to repair the fiscal 1982 budget left behind by the Carter Administration called for spending cuts *lower than those mandated for fiscal 1987 by Congress's own Gramm-Rudman Act.* But along with some frightening but manageable spending cuts came the real centerpiece of Mr. Reagan's economic program, the Kemp-Roth tax cuts. With individual income tax collections down and corporate tax collections virtually non-existent, even a doubling of the national debt couldn't produce the revenues needed to fund bureaucracy as usual. Since more dollars found their way to the Pentagon, the revenue reduction was felt particularly acutely in the same domestic programs year after year. Now Gramm-Rudman imposes even more cuts, some in the very same places, and it, too, is really a part of the Reagan fallout. One doubts that Congress would have chosen such a crude device to deal with the $30–50 billion deficits we would have faced in the absence of the Reagan tax cuts.

No one can question Mr. Reagan's impact on bureaucratic

budgets. Although his 1981–82 supply side promise that the tax cuts would not drastically reduce government revenues makes it impossible to know if he expected to have this sort of impact, he hardly seems disappointed by it. But it's going to be a long time before any President gets an opportunity to change government's overall revenue picture that drastically. In addition, Mr. Reagan believed then, and apparently still does, that, outside of the Pentagon, every agency has too much money to spend. This budgetary equivalent of a "Nuke 'Em!" strategy would be far less appealing to someone who thought some agencies had too much and others too little. In any case, appealing or not, it appears to be foreclosed for the foreseeable future.

If we rule out another pre-emptive strike on total revenues, can a President have much effect on an agency's budget and through that budget an agency's ability to pursue its policy objectives? He can, but there are some pretty powerful constraints on how much and what kind of effect he can have.

First, three dollars out of every four spent by the federal government fall in that category budget makers call the uncontrollables. They are spent to pay interest on the national debt, purchase weapons systems or spare parts contracted for in previous years, or sent to those deemed to be entitled to receive them. We really can't avoid spending these dollars, save in the entitlement programs, of course, and there we can only hold back the spending by changing the statutory basis of the entitlement. Early in the Reagan Administration we were told that the price support programs for wheat, corn, and soybeans would cost less than $5 billion for fiscal 1983. They cost more than twice that when the year ended. The reason for the discrepancy lay in some very optimistic forecasts of commodity prices for that particular year. The budgeted number notwithstanding, the additional dollars had to be paid out since Congress wasn't about to declare farmers ineligible retroactively. One doubts the courts would have permitted it to do so anyway. Unless a President can convince authorizing committees of Congress to alter many of these entitlement programs and their dollar allocation formulas, or gets a Reagan-like opportunity to cut all revenues substantially, it appears that there isn't that much he can do to affect a whole lot of the budget and a whole lot of agencies.

Second, the document is massive, and time, knowledge, and interest are in short supply. The career examiners at OMB are probably less fiercely independent than they were in their 1950's and 1960's heydays, but they are hardly dutiful presidential servants, putting his stamp on every agency and program that comes by. An awful lot of what goes to Congress in the President's budget got there without his knowledge, let alone participation and approval. It couldn't be otherwise.

Finally, Congress is still pretty serious about the budget-making business and whatever a President wants to do to/for a particular agency has to get by Congress somewhere along the line. Every year, eight out of ten executive branch agencies end up with more or less money to spend than the President told them they would have, so there can be no doubt that Congress does make some alterations in the Chief's spending blueprint. He wins some and he loses some but there is no questioning the fact that congressional power is one more constraint on the President's use of the budget as a means to influence bureaucracy.

These are powerful limitations, but they don't quite put the President in a budgetary straightjacket. Three-fourths of the budget may be pretty well tied up, but the other one-fourth goes through the traditional appropriations process. The Chief can check on proposed expenditures for any agencies he is particularly interested in and move these numbers up or down before the budget goes to Congress. He can't cover all of the agencies that dip into this quarter of the budget, but since he doesn't care about a lot of them or what they are doing anyway, his inability to scan it all is a minor nuisance but not a major worry. Once the budget goes to Congress he can prod, negotiate, and trade to keep the cuts/increases he has settled on for some agencies. He won't win all of them, but he won't lose all of them either.

In sum, a President who wants to go after a carefully selected handful of agencies and programs can probably influence how much money they will have to spend. Likewise, the President who wanted to see that every agency had less to spend got his wish. By gutting the whole revenue system, Mr. Reagan hit everybody's budget. But a President who wants to have a systematic, policy-specific impact, one who wants to move some agency budgets up and some down, but wants to have an effect on all of them, is doomed to failure. Of course, no such President is likely to exist anyway, so given the more limited goal of selective intervention, the budget gives the Chief some definite leverage over bureaucracy.

Summary and Conclusion

"The race is not always to the swift nor the battle to the strong. But, that's definitely the way to bet." Damon Runyon's sage advice is easily adapted to the struggle between the President and the federal bureaucracy. The battle does not always go to the bureaucrats, but if an agency is pursuing policies that aren't in line with presidential priorities, bet on the agency. At least that's sound advice if all you know is that an agency is doing things inconsistent with a President's preferences. If you know a little more, however, you can start to do some handicapping, and what Damon Runyon character could resist the opportunity to outsmart the cautious bettor?

The first thing to try to find out is whether or not the President knows this particular agency is operating at odds with his preferences. This is really a two-part question. Does the Chief have any preferences about what this agency does and has he got any information about what it is doing? As I've said repeatedly in this chapter, both answers are probably No. How could any human being reasonably be expected to have strong feelings about the tremendous number of issues confronted by the executive branch of government? Even if a President does care about an issue, information doesn't always flow very effectively from the "bottom" of the executive branch toward the top and the expertise to interpret a lot of that information isn't there anyway. As if that isn't enough, who at the top has the time to look at it. Presidents rarely care and are even less likely to know and understand, but when they do, the odds begin to shift. It's not time to take money out of your savings account so you can make the big score, but it is time to hustle up some more information.

The next thing you'd better try to find out is whether the agency is doing something the President doesn't want it to do or not doing something he does want it to do. If it is the latter he has a real problem on his hands, but if it is the former, the cautious bettor is a large step closer to taking a fall.

If the President wants to get an agency to do something new, there is little he can do but try to persuade. If the agency lacks the authority to do it, he first must persuade Congress to grant such authority, then convince the agency to use it. If the agency has the authority and just isn't using it, the President's job is easier, but there is probably a reason why it isn't using that piece of its legal mandate in that way and, given the normal bureaucratic suspicion of presidential intervention, he's going to have a tough time convincing most agencies to embark on a new, presidentially designed, course. He may have to get the agency the money to head off in new directions and, even if he succeeds in getting it, he's got to find some way to make sure that is where the money goes. It isn't going to be easy. What it all boils down to, of course, is the one simple fact that the President's tools don't lend themselves to getting an agency to go somewhere new. His appointees have trouble leading agencies in new directions. It is hard to get an agency new authority and it can be even harder to make sure the agency uses it the way the President wants it used. Even budgets don't work very well since the Chief has to get the money out of Congress and be sure it is spent in the way he wants it spent. If the President's problem with an agency centers on something he wants it to start doing, keep your money on the bureaucrats.

If, on the other hand, the President wants to stop something, it is time to give some careful thought to switching sides. Now the Chief is pretty much an even money bet. The blocking tools at his disposal are generally effective. The next several Presidents almost certainly won't be able to repeat Ronald Reagan's successful attack on the whole revenue system, but they will probably be able to cut selectively and the policy consequences of dollars denied are generally more predictable than those of dollars granted. Pulling authority away from an agency is tough, but denying it new authority is pretty easy and that particular power can fairly readily be used as a "bargaining chip." Reorganization is harder to use than it used to be, and it never was all that easy. The actual reorganization plans lost as often as they won. But the energy expended by an agency in fending off these presidential initiatives, combined with the political capital the bureaucrats were forced to use up during the fight, will slow that agency down. Finally, a President who wants to slow/stop/frustrate an agency can use his appointment powers to see to it that the agency is in a constant battle with its departmental overseers. Again, the drain on an agency's energy and political capital can be enormous, and the agency's ability to pursue the policies the Chief opposes is bound to be reduced. James Watt may not have been the devil his opponents claimed, but career bureaucrats at Interior spent an awful lot of time and spilled a good deal of their own blood in keeping him from doing all of the things he wanted to do. In the process, they couldn't do all they wanted to do either.

The frustrations felt by the National Park Service over the past few years are a perfect illustration of what a President can do to prevent an agency from going where it wants to go. Ronald Reagan may not be the environmental disaster his critics paint him, but it is reasonable to say that he is anything but an aggressive proponent of more parks with tighter restrictions on how those parks are used. A general pro-business, pro-development, pro-private control preference, along with a conviction that every agency was spending too much money, worked to convince him to oppose further land acquisitions for the National Park System. His successful attack on the whole budget meant that money for land acquisition would be hard to come by. His appointees at the top of the Interior Department were just as opposed to a bigger, more tightly controlled park system as he was so they refused to approve Park Service requests for acquisition dollars. The Service managed to convince Congress to put some in anyway, but the amount was far below what Park Service leaders felt was needed and the President's fiscal 1987 budget even proposed recissions of much of that money.

Even after Reagan's surprise appointment of respected conservationist William Penn Mott as Director of the Park Service, things stayed pretty much the same. Mott did an awful lot of proposing, including a "Tall Grass Prairie" park in Oklahoma and a protected scenic highway the length of the Big Sur country, but his bosses have said, "Great, when we finally find the money." They haven't looked very hard. Beyond that, one of those bosses, William Horn, Assistant Secretary of Interior for Fish and Wildlife and Parks, ordered Mott to reconsider his proposed restrictions on off-road vehicle use on the Cape Cod Seashore and to cancel a speech at a "Save the Everglades" conference scheduled for January 1986 in Florida. Mott is a good soldier. He did both. He also dropped the Big Sur Highway proposal in favor of "local initiatives" to protect that stretch of California coastline.[56]

You can add some more refinements to your handicapping system if you want to. For example, you could find out about the President's current political health as well as the amount and type of support the agency has in Congress and with the kinds of organized interest groups that traditionally support career bureaucrats when they struggle with their executive branch bosses. You could add in the personal and professional prestige of agency leadership and even the nature of the policy area in which the agency toils. In fact you could do an awful lot of fine tuning if you plan to figure the odds on every contest. But, if you do not intend to make a career of it, find out if the President cares about a particular policy area and knows what the agency or agencies responsible for that area are doing. If he doesn't, put your money on the bureaucrats. If he does, find out what is bothering him about the agency's activities. If he wants it to do something it isn't currently doing, keep your money where it is. But it's OK to be a little nervous. If, on the other hand, he wants an agency to stop doing what it is doing, or at least to do less of it, it is time to give serious thought to changing your bet. The President still may lose, but he stands a pretty good chance of winning since the means at his disposal are well suited to an effort to slow down or stop even the most determined of agencies. Indeed, maybe the best advice in these situations is Don't bet. Just watch the game and enjoy.

So the President does have some influence over the federal bureaucracy. It is hardly systematic or pervasive, and he can use it far more effectively to slow an agency than he can to prod it. Still, influence it is and Presidents do sometimes use it. But what is the impact of this influence—or lack of influence—on our efforts to keep bureaucracy in line with democratic values? Where does the Chief lead his bureaucrats?

The normal situation—a lack of presidential influence over agency decision making—means bureaucracy guided by its own view of sound policy and subject to the influence of Congress and the public. As we shall see in the next two chapters, that means a very narrow view of the public interest and a resulting decision-making system dominated by organized interest groups and professional associations.

When the President tries, and particularly when he succeeds, it ought to be different. After all, he is elected and the bureaucrats are not, and he is the only elected official we have with a claim to a national majority as his constituency. On the other hand, we all know that elections speak to most issues in vague and general terms, if, indeed, they speak to most issues at all. I don't know what the American public would say if asked whether or not we ought to expand the national park system. I am quite certain, however, that in electing Ronald Reagan in 1980 and re-electing him four years later, that public was not trying to answer that particular question. To be sure, anyone who thought a vote for Mr. Reagan in 1984 would lead to an expanded park system had a pretty strange reading of the previous four years of budgetary and environmental decisions, but I doubt the future of the parks was uppermost in many minds in the summer and fall of 1984.

Now then, everybody ready for the big cop out? The answer to the question of whether or not presidential influence leads toward democratic values is that it is a matter of opinion.

Elections are the basic legitimizing agent in a democratic society and the President is the only elected official we have who can claim a national constituency. That doesn't entitle him to break the law or disregard the Constitution—court decisions are powerful legitimizers, too—nor does it entitle him to run roughshod over a true congressional majority. That's a national majority of its own. But it does give him an awful big dose of legitimacy when confronting bureaucrats backed only by a highly unrepresentative congressional subcommittee and one or two organized interest groups.

Standing against that legitimacy is the uncomfortable reality of our presidential elections. By their very nature, they could not possibly speak to the myriad of issues that might divide the Chief from the various agencies. Democracy is more than translating majority preferences into public policy anyway, but there can be no doubt that the President's claim that he speaks for a national majority on most of the questions that bureaucrats must answer rests on pretty shaky ground.

In the end, then, it comes down to this. If you believe that a President who stays within the law and the Constitution and compromises with real congressional majorities ought to be allowed to do more or less as he pleases, then when the President wins, democracy wins. If you believe that elections speak only to general policy directions and, consequently, that the Chief's claim to speak for a national majority on any particular issue is highly suspect, then when the President wins, democracy may win or lose. The problem is finding a standard—other than one's own preference on the issue—that will provide the answer.

Bureaucracy and the Congress

C ongress cannot lay claim to the title Chief Executive, but the Constitution does give it the power to pass laws and appropriate money for the conduct of government, and since bureaucrats are the ones who carry out those laws and spend that money, Congress is bound to look for some way to influence bureaucratic decision making. Unlike the President, the Congress has found it.

In the first place, Congress has a pretty good idea of what most agencies are doing most of the time. Second, Congress has an arsenal of weapons sufficient to induce even bureau chiefs to be "looking over their shoulders . . . at the elements of the legislative establishment relevant to their agencies—taking stock of moods and attitudes, estimating reactions to contemplated decisions and actions, trying to prevent misunderstandings and avoidable conflicts, and planning responses when storm warnings appeared on the horizon."[1] Finally, the resistance that faces the President is replaced by a pattern of cooperation between agency careerists and the staff and membership of the congressional committees or subcommittees that operate in that agency's policy area.

Mutual Attraction: Self-interest and Empathy

Congressional committees and subcommittees generally get along quite well with the executive branch agencies within their respective policy domains. Each has a great deal to gain from cooperation, and it even feels good since they turn out to be so much alike.

Mutual Self-interest

Close and cooperative working relationships with "their" subcommittees provide agencies with two indispensable benefits. The first is power. The second is legitimacy, legitimacy for both the power they possess and the policies they produce.

As noted in Chapter 1, the politician side of the bureaucrat recognizes and accepts the fact that politics plays a role in the formulation of public policy. If bureaucrats are going to enter the political arena they will need to bring along some of the coin of the realm—that is, they will need power. Knowledge provides some, but not enough, so bureaucrats must find an expressly political base of power. On four key dimensions—longevity, expertise, sympathy for agency support groups, and power itself—congressional committees and subcommittees are an ideal place to look.

Congressional subcommittees can rarely match the expertise of executive branch agencies, but they are hardly amateurs, particularly not when compared to the President and his appointees. Several of the subcommittee members themselves are likely to be legitimate policy experts, and Hugh Heclo notes that in the hiring of personal and committee staff there is a trend toward an individual likely to be "skilled in dealing with certain complex policy issues, possibly with credentials as a policy analyst, but certainly an expert in using other experts and their networks." [2] A handful of experts among the membership backed up by a fairly knowledgeable staff can create something akin to a professional atmosphere as the committee considers the policy and/ or budgetary issues before it. Again, subcommittees cannot match bureaucratic expertise, but at the very least both sides speak the same — technical — language, accept the legitimacy of the same kinds of data, and generally respect the same sets of people.

In addition to being fairly knowledgeable, subcommittees are rather stable operations. There is more turnover among the membership of Congress today than there was a decade or two ago, but every committee has a core of members who have been around a long time and a group who will be. Turnover is far higher among congressional staff people than among the membership, of course, since lots of ambitious young men and women seek out such staff jobs precisely because of their value in landing some other job a few years down the road. On the other hand, a recent study of congressional staffs suggests that not everyone is there to put an important line on his or her vita. Using a measuring device they labeled "mean committee half-life," Robert Salisbury and Kenneth Shepsle found considerable stability among the staffs of House and Senate committees.[3] To simplify it a bit, Salisbury and Shepsle looked at the new staff hires for each committee for each year from 1962 through 1978. Then they followed each freshman class to see how long it took before half of them had left the committee staff. Averaging the numbers produced the mean committee half-life for each committee.

Some committees showed remarkable turnover. The House Small Business Committee lost half of its new hires within two years, and even the prestigious House Appropriations Committee lost them in two and one-half.[4] But the Interior Committee still had half of each class after 4.4 years, Agriculture after 5.4, and Armed Services a remarkable 7.7.[5] As Salisbury and Shepsle point out, the probability that any congressional staffer will leave his or her post peaks at four years, then goes down substantially and levels off until staffers approach the magic twenty years for retirement benefits.[6] That suggests that an awful lot of that 50 percent of the Agriculture Committee's class of 1970 that was still around in 1975 planned on digging in for the long haul. Thirteen of the twenty-two House committees had average half-lives of four years or more. It may not be the kind of permanence that we find among agency careerists, but between the members and the staff, nearly all of Congress's committees can be considered pretty stable. This sort of continuity reduces the likelihood of drastic changes in programs and policies and means someone else will have to face the long-term consequences of any changes that are made.

As we shall see in the next chapter, executive branch agencies establish close working relationships with certain segments of the American public. Based on personal ties and professional (knowledge-based) commitments as well as political necessity, these agency-supporter ties are powerful and enduring. Agency personnel don't want to do anything that could possibly disrupt them. Close cooperation with the relevant subcommittees won't threaten these ties, since these subcommittees are almost as closely linked to agency support groups as are the agencies themselves.

The most enduring of the subcommittee interest group ties are probably those grounded in observable constituency interest. Individuals who represent constituencies in which one or two industries dominate the economic landscape seek, and generally receive, assignments to committees and subcommittees whose activities will have some impact on the economic health of those industries.[7] Three-fourths of the members of the House Agriculture Committee represent districts in which the percentage of people directly employed in agricultural production is more than twice the national average, and a working majority of the Committee comes from districts in which at least one person out of every ten is in the farming business. Over 80 percent of the House Merchant Marine and Fisheries Committee represent coastal, Great Lakes, ship-building or port districts, while the Interior Committees of both houses retain slim working majorities of Westerners, generally sympathetic to the traditional—and some of the newer—uses and users of the public lands of the Interior West. This constituency connection extends to the subcommittee level, most noticeably in the commodity-based subcommittee system of the House and Senate Agriculture Committees, but also in lesser-known spots like the Subcommittee on Transportation, Aviation and Materials, chaired by Dan Glickman (D. Kan), whose Wichita district is home to the largest Boeing plant outside of the Seattle metropolitan area as well as to the major manufacturing operations of Cessna, Beechcraft, and Piper, the three leading producers of small aircraft in the United States.[8]

Campaign contributions constitute a second source for subcommittee interest group bonds. These groups, or more properly the Political Action Committees they create for the purpose, can and do supply congressional candidates with large sums of money for campaign purposes. More important than the total number of dollars such groups put into congressional campaign coffers, is the targeting of these dollars. Interest group leaders understand the power of these legislative subunits—Committee opposition means almost certain defeat, Committee support goes a long way toward ensuring victory—and they direct group money where it will do the most good. The AMA sees that its dollars go to Ways and Means members (Medicare and Medicaid), just as the NEA finds the Education and Labor Committee, the Maritime Unions and their shipping industry bosses find Merchant Marine and Fisheries, and so on.[9]

Beyond votes and dollars, these interest groups can supply committees and subcommittees with information and the expertise to interpret that information. Obviously such groups can supply vital political information—how will this particular action be received by the people most likely to know and care about it—but Dennis Ippolito and Thomas Walker found subcommittees relying on these groups for technical information as well.[10] Such information may well be slanted and the experts who provide it biased, but the members of Congress and interest group leaders they talked to convinced Ippolito and Walker that "these research reports are written in a fashion supportive of the group's policy objectives, but to maintain credibility with the committee, the information must be of sound quality."[11]

Whether based on constituency, dollars, expertise, or all three, the point is this. The congressional committees and subcommittees with jurisdiction over a particular area of policy and the agency or agencies that operate within it are highly sympathetic to the support groups aligned with those agencies. Consequently, close cooperation with their subcommittees will not threaten the interests these agencies have chosen to protect. That makes such cooperation all the more attractive.

Finally, as I noted in the beginning of this chapter, these subcommittees have enough power to be able to cause bureau chiefs to "look over their shoulders."[12] They also have the power to shape legislation, influence budgets, head off embarrassing investigations, move programs, reassign agencies, and even frustrate the President of the United States.

Subcommittees make an excellent power base. The price of that power is cooperation—that is, agencies have to allow subcommittee influence over their decisions—but given the key characteristics of expertise, longevity, and sympathy for the right people, it is a small price paid willingly.

Along with power, agencies gain legitimacy through close cooperation with congressional subcommittees. The American commitment to democracy demands that anyone who exercises governmental power be able to demonstrate a rightful claim to its possession and use. Since all power is supposed to flow from the people, the normal means for legitimizing it is by holding an election. But this puts bureaucrats in an awkward position, since they are not elected and it is virtually impossible to see how they could be or why they should be. Their power must be legitimized indirectly and the logical vehicle for doing so is a close working relationship with someone whose power is clearly and directly legitimate. In effect, agency staff can now say, "These policies were formulated with congressional (obviously legitimate) participation. Members of Congress approve of the policies and they approve of us and, should that approval cease, they can and will take corrective action."

At first glance it may appear that legitimacy is mere window dressing, a nice little extra benefit from the agency-committee relationship, but hardly essential to it. In the short run, for a specific decision, power clearly is more important than legitimacy, but over the long haul, any agency widely and consistently perceived as illegitimate is headed for trouble. Even the FBI and the CIA felt the sting of revealing—and embarrassing—investigations and found themselves subject to increased congressional scrutiny and control largely because each was perceived as having consistently pursued policies that it and it alone had formulated. Besides, bureaucrats, too, are committed to democratic norms, including the central notion of government by the people, and how can one justify a challenge to the policies of one legitimate power holder (the President) except by referring to those of another (the Congress)?

Subcommittee members, too, gain substantial benefits by working closely and cooperatively with executive branch agencies. Specifically, they can use this cooperative relationship and the influence it brings them within bureaucracy to enhance their chances for re-election, move public policy in the direction they believe best, and secure some measure of influence within their particular legislative chamber. From the perspective of an individual member of Congress, that is a very attractive prospect.[13]

Most members of Congress are well aware that the laws they pass are rather like skeletons, sometimes not very well-developed skeletons at that. Congress can, and has, said it ought to be safe to work in a textile mill, but it wasn't about to say whether a cotton dust rule or masks for workers was the better way to make it safe, and it was even less likely to try to specify the timetable for compliance with either means for a particular mill belonging to a particular company. It was/is OSHA's job to handle these "administrative" questions.

Congress as a whole may be happy to delegate these and thousands of other questions to bureaucrats, but specific members of Congress want to keep an eye on, sometimes even a hand in, the action. The reasons are two. Such questions can have a significant impact on a member's re-election chances, and they are critical to the success of a particular policy.

If, whether by dint of constituency or campaign contributions, a member of Congress is called upon to represent the textile industry, that representation will be ever so much more effective if that member can extend his or her influence to the issue of rules versus masks, or the question of when and how a particular mill must comply. The same can be said for members who want to protect the interests of farmers, shippers, users of public land and its resources, or defense contractors. Close and cooperative agency-committee relationships are the means by which individual members exercise influence over these kinds of decisions. As Lawrence Dodd and Richard Schott conclude: "From the standpoint of individual members, this increased access to the subsystem arena carried personal advantage. It gave more of them an opportunity to develop close ties to key interest groups and to key bureaucratic agencies. . . . *It goes almost without saying that these close ties bring electoral benefits.*" [14]

Electoral advantage is not the only reason for a member of Congress to want the influence that generally comes with a close working relationship with a specific executive branch agency. Anyone who cares about the ongoing quest for safe and healthy work places cares about the decisions between masks and dust rules, earplugs and noise reduction, respirators and lower gas and particulate levels, and hundreds of others like them. He or she also cares about compliance timetables for thousands of individual factories. Only when all of these specific implementing decisions are added up will we really know what our occupational health and safety policy is, what price we paid to get it, and who was called upon to pay that price. If a member wants to influence that policy, he or she must influence these implementing decisions and, once again, cooperative agency-subcommittee relationships are the vehicle for doing so.

Finally, a member may be able to use a close relationship with a particular agency to increase his or her influence within the Congress. For most members, this particular goal ranks well below those of re-election and the ability to move public policy in the right direction. Still, for some it counts, and cooperation with bureaucracy helps those members obtain it. Part of this increased internal influence comes from favor trading—that is, from helping a colleague with a problem with "your" agency and holding the IOU. Far more important is the ability to use an agency to gain an informal education in a particular policy area, then, subsequently, as a continuous information service. A member who diligently does his or her homework and consistently displays an easy command of the facts can earn the designation expert, and with it a certain amount of recognition, prestige, and eventually influence. Bureaucrats can help.

In short, agencies derive considerable power—from a nearly ideal source at that—and a sense of legitimacy, and subcommittee members, in turn, gain influence over agency decisions and with that influence comes the opportunity to produce the kind of public policy the member believes is best, a measure of influence within his or her legislative chamber, and political support that can almost certainly be used to enhance re-election prospects. With that much to gain on each side, anything other than a close and cooperative relationship between the two would be a mystery.

Empathy

Self-interest is the primary reason for the closeness of the agency-subcommittee relationship, but empathy, too, plays a role. Congressional subcommittees and bureaucratic agencies get along so well in part because the individual members of the subcommittees and the professionals who staff the agencies have a great deal in common.

On a general level, there are the powerful bonds of longevity and expertise. Both sides view the making of public policy as a continuous evolutionary process requiring specialized knowledge and constant effort and attention. They tend to be highly suspicious of anyone whose attitude differs from theirs—Presidents and Cabinet Secretaries, for example—and drawn to those who share it. Further, as Dodd and Schott point out, "For both members of Congress and the federal bureaucracy government is a career—in contrast to the 'in and out' patterns of the political appointees." [15] People with career orientations, a long-term focus, and a conviction that they, and they alone, have the knowledge needed to decide the questions at hand have a strong tie to one another, and that tie is bound to cement an already friendly relationship.

Turning from the general to the specific, that is, looking at a particular subcommittee and "its" agency, we find a further bond, common background. The vast majority of the top and middle-level careerists at the Department of Agriculture are the products of Midwestern farms or small towns and were educated in land grant colleges. So are most of the members of the House Agriculture Committee. We find the same similarity at Interior and elsewhere. Even if their paths have never actually crossed, an Agricultural Stabilization and Conservation Service bureaucrat from Ottumwa, Iowa, by way of Iowa State University, has a great deal in common with a House member from Aberdeen, South Dakota, and South Dakota State. They will sense it, and it will draw them together, even as it separates them from the folks from New York and Boston.

By itself, empathy would not produce agency-subcommittee ties as close as those we frequently find. But it does provide a supplement to the self-interest connection and probably makes the ties closer and more durable. Agencies and subcommittees need each other, so cooperation is inevitable. But it is ever so much nicer to establish these working relationships with someone "pretty much like us."

All is not sweetness and light in the land of agency-subcommittee relationships. The two can get into some real donnybrooks. Family fights, after all, are sometimes the bloodiest of all. But the bonds of self-interest and empathy are powerful. Cooperation is the norm, conflict the exception, and, as a result, one major barrier to external influence—bureaucratic resistance—is lowered.

What's Going On Over There?

Congressional efforts to gather information about bureaucratic performance have become an important part of the legislative process. Though we often lump all of these information-gathering efforts together under the single heading oversight, the Legislative Reorganization Act of 1946 specifies three different types of congressional oversight over bureaucracy and, in keeping with institutional custom, is careful to assign primary responsibility for each to different congressional committees.[16] The Appropriations Committees are given the task of fiscal oversight, that is, of making sure that money is spent in the way Congress wants it spent. Authorization committees are charged with legislative oversight or the responsibility for determining "whether particular programs work and . . . proposing remedies to problems they uncover."[17] Finally, the Government Operations Committees are assigned the task of investigative oversight, that is, "a mandate for wide ranging inquiry into government economy, efficiency, and effectiveness."[18]

Neat as this division may be in the law, there is considerable overlap among the three in practice, creating the potential for some real battles among the various committees. Still, these are different types of oversight conducted by different people with different goals and perspectives, so each must be considered separately, even as we recognize the potential for overlap, confusion, and internal congressional conflicts. I prefer to discuss legislative and investigative oversight here, leaving fiscal oversight for the section on the budget, since it appears as if Congress has begun to rely increasingly upon this tool as a means of coping with the chaos of the current budget-making game.

Legislative Oversight

Legislative oversight is the province of the authorizing committees, but, as one would expect, has been shifted down to the subcommittee level. A good many of the House committees have created separate oversight or investigation subcommittees. The Senate generally has not followed suit, and one suspects that a good many of the substantive subcommittees in the House are still doing something suspiciously like oversight. In any event, subcommittees acquire information about bureaucratic performance formally and informally, deliberately and accidentally, but they do acquire it.

Probably the most important sources of information about bureaucratic policy making are the agencies themselves. Informal give and take about what agencies are doing, what they expect to do, and how well they feel policies are working is an integral part of the close and cooperative working relationship that both sides find so beneficial. An agency official who feels that a particular policy may not be working as had been hoped, or who simply wants to confirm his or her interpretation of the law, will check in with key subcommittee members or staff. Herbert Kaufman found one of the bureaus he studied to be so receptive to this sort of informal contact that, in response to a Senate committee request to know more about a particular aspect of agency operations, it literally allowed committee staffers to move in and watch.[19] It is easy to see why agencies themselves would become primary suppliers of information about their activities. Relationships with their subcommittees could hardly remain close if they refused such contact, and the rewards can be immediate and tangible. After all, as Aaron Wildavsky reports, no less zealous a budgetary guardian than the late Congressman John Rooney (D. N.Y.) took time out from a budget hearing to compliment an agency head for his policy of keeping the subcommittee posted on agency activities even when its budget was not pending.[20] In any case, formal means for finding out are on the back shelf and can always be dusted off and used.

Before we consider these formal mechanisms, however, there are two other informal sources of information about bureaucratic performance, and while they are less important than the informal agency-subcommittee give and take, they do provide Congress with some additional insight into what is happening at the various agencies. Specifically, subcommittees gather some information about agency activity from communications with individual constituents and with the representatives of organized interest groups.

Interest groups provide a constant source of feedback on agency activity. Some of this communication is formalized through reports or testimony at subcommittee hearings, but a good bit remains informal and behind the scenes as a normal part of the ongoing relationship between congressional subcommittees and the groups active within their areas of responsibility. If the National Association of Cotton Growers is unhappy with the Agricultural Stabilization and Conservation Service, the Cotton, Rice, and Sugar Subcommittee of the House Agriculture Committee will hear about it, just as Merchant Marine and Fisheries will hear about maritime industry frustration with the Federal Maritime Commission, the Forests, Family Farms, and Energy Subcommittee will find out if Weyerhauser and Georgia Pacific are mad at the Forest Service, and so on. Such communications may well be biased, but subcommittee-interest group ties are firmly established and listening to such complaints and taking the offending agency to task are one element of the job the subcommittee has assumed as its part of the bargain.

Last, and for once least, is the information that comes from individual constituents. Such information is nearly always negative and case specific, and members of Congress almost never seek to put such cases in a general perspective or use them to gather systematic information about implementation of a particular policy by a particular agency. In addition, the vast majority of such citizen complaints concern routine matters—except to the one complaining, of course—such as foreign travel (Where is my passport?), immigration (It's about my cousin Giovanni!), or a check that didn't end up where it was supposed to or appears to be for the wrong amount. Many of these are handled in an almost perfunctory manner and rarely do agencies change their minds about the proper course of action. There are exceptions, such as the mid-seventies discovery that the Pentagon had been using coded discharge numbers to brand former servicemen as drug users, homosexuals, or just plain trouble makers, or the parallel finding of serious Veterans Administration bungling in the processing of veterans benefits claims.[21] In both cases, Congress was moved to act. Still, in general, communications from individual constituents are a distant third as a way for subcommittees to monitor agency activity.

Not all of the information that flows to congressional committees and subcommittees comes informally. These legislative subunits hold lots and lots of hearings and require more and more executive branch agencies to submit more and more reports. Both the hearings and the reports can reveal a good bit about agency performance.

Between 1947 and 1970, the various committees of the Congress held nearly 15,000 hearings,[22] and two recent studies indicate that the frequency of such hearings actually increased during the subsequent decade.[23] Monitoring bureaucratic implementation of policy decisions is only one of many reasons to call a committee hearing, and, according to Lawrence Dodd, George Shipley, and Philip Diehl, fewer than one-third of the 15,000 hearings held between 1947 and 1970 focused on such questions.[24] Still the names of key bureaucrats are present on the witness lists of a high proportion of these hearings — Herbert Kaufman reports that, during the 95th Congress alone, representatives of the Food and Drug Administration made eighty-five separate appearances at committee hearings[25] — and, therefore, even if the bulk of any particular hearing was devoted to broad policy concerns, the opportunity to shift the focus to agency or program specific concerns was almost always present.

Kaufman's description of the kind of preparation engaged in by bureau chiefs about to appear at committee hearings leaves the clear impression that these men felt they should be prepared for anything. "Bureau experts in the matters under consideration assembled briefing books covering every topic that might arise at hearings. . . . Just before the appearance, the functional specialists and the chief held briefing sessions, each specialist going over his part of the bureau's responsibilities. The chief followed along in the briefing book, asking questions to make sure he was in command of the subject."[26] Even this much preparation was not always deemed sufficient, for, as Kaufman goes on to say, "when a chief appeared, he was usually accompanied by specialists who either furnished him with the information needed to answer committee inquiries or were permitted to answer directly."[27]

We cannot conclude that even this astounding number of hearings generated a steady supply of detailed information about bureaucratic implementation of policy decisions, but neither must we conclude that the subcommittees found out nothing. Rather, it seems that most of these hearings provided the opportunity for an interested member of the committee or its staff to ask some program-related questions and gather program-related information and that agency staff felt they had better be able to supply the answers.

Finally, there are the reports. There are annual reports, issue or problem specific reports, even some management reports, and before the Supreme Court stepped in, all agencies subject to legislative veto were required to inform Congress (or one of its committees) of proposed actions that might fall under that veto provision.[28] As a means of communicating information about bureaucratic performance, however, formal agency reports suffer from a couple of relatively serious defects. In the first place, they don't always get read. Certain committee staffers may monitor the reports in their individual areas of specialization, and given the individualized and idiosyncratic nature of a good deal of subcommittee activity, that one reading might spur further inquiry and even action. Still, Morris Ogul is probably right when he concludes that most reports do not get wide enough circulation or serious enough attention to be considered a major source of congressional information about bureaucracy.[29] Second, a formal report may well be far more "sanitized" than hearing testimony or informal agency-subcommittee contacts. Informal communications are in some sense off the record and among friends, and hearings are under oath and only partially rehearsed. Reports are agency documents, carefully edited, often by more than one staff member. Testimony at hearings is rehearsed and edited, but it is harder to edit as one is speaking, especially when trying to do so under oath and on congressional turf rather than over a familiar desk writing one more report.

Hearings, reports, complaints from constituents and organized interest groups, and, most importantly, informal contacts of all sorts give authorizing committees access to a lot of information about agency policy making. Because so much flows informally —thus leaving no observable trail—it is difficult to determine how much these committees know about their agencies, but Robert Stein and James Regans were convinced that the 91st and 94th Congresses had used subcommittee hearings to increase both the quantity and the quality of its formal oversight activities dramatically,[30] and there is every reason to believe that more goes on behind the scenes than in front. Authorizing committees may know less about bureaucracy than their critics feel they should. On occasion they probably even know less than they would like to know. Still, I am convinced that these committees and subcommittees have the capacity to find out about bureaucratic activity, that they use it, and that it puts these legislative subunits in a position from which they can exercise considerable influence over their agencies and the policies they pursue.

Investigative Oversight

I suspect that a good many of us, when we think of oversight, harbor thoughts of dedicated members of Congress and diligent staffers ferreting out bureaucratic wrong doing. In short, a lot of us probably think of investigative oversight. It can be headline grabbing—remember hearing about the $2,000 coffee pot or the secret bombing of Cambodia or CIA misdeeds—but, in reality, not all that many Woodward and Bernstein clones are to be found on congressional staffs, and investigative oversight is the least prevalent and the least effective of the three types of oversight Congress attempts to conduct.

The Legislative Reorganization Act of 1946 lodges responsibility for investigative oversight in the Government Operations Committees of the House and Senate. Despite a formal grant of what would appear to be some rather formidable powers,[31] these committees have never realized the potential for effective investigative oversight envisioned for them three and one-half decades ago by congressional reformers. Three powerful forces have prevented them from doing so.

To begin with, Government Operations Committees cannot legislate. They can investigate, they can even come to some conclusions about personnel or policy changes that ought to be made based on what their investigations reveal. But they cannot turn those conclusions into law. Instead, they must send the information they have gathered and any recommendations they wish to make to the authorizing committee with jurisdiction over this particular policy area. Any legislative remedy must originate there. This militates against really effective oversight in two interrelated ways. First, agency officials have less incentive to cooperate with the Government Operations Committees—that is, to supply information, comply with informal suggestions, and so forth—since the agencies know that legislative action will not be taken until their authorization committee is ready to take it. Second, the lack of real legislative authority dampens the investigatory enthusiasm of GOC members and staff. Why go all out to gather information and prepare a blueprint for more effective policy implementation when both will just be turned over to someone else, especially to someone else unlikely to pay much attention?

Second, there is a good bit of animosity between the two Government Operations Committees and the authorization committees and subcommittees of their respective chambers. GOC members often see authorization committees as agency partisans unwilling and/or unable to see problems and solutions, while authorization committee members see GOC people as dilettantes, unfamiliar with program and policy details, just doing a little "headline hunting" at the expense of agencies trying to do a job. The balance of power tips so heavily in favor of the authorization committees that the Government Operations Committees have been forced to "be especially sensitive to the expectations and demands of the larger body." [32] In less flattering terms, to keep enough dollars to operate and to get any sort of hearing for their recommendations, they have had to tone down their investigations, stay in constant contact with authorization committee members, and generally play by the rules those committees want to impose.

Finally, it is almost impossible to imagine agency officials and GOC members entering into the kind of close and cooperative working relationships that are common between such officials and the members of authorization committees. The bonds of common background, the shared knowledge, and the representation of similar interests simply are not there. On top of that, the bureaucrat soon concludes that the Government Operations Committees can do his or her agency some harm, but not very much good. This lack of a cooperative working relationship between the GOC's and the agencies hinders the former's oversight efforts. Recall that just such relationships aided legislative oversight by establishing informal channels of communication and influence every bit as effective as the formal channels they supplement. Such channels almost never exist for the Government Operations Committees—it is hard to see how they could since investigative oversight is by its nature adversarial—and their absence weakens the committees and frustrates their oversight efforts.

The Government Operations Committees do do some digging and they occasionally hit pay dirt. But without informal communications channels and constrained by the fear of offending authorization committees by overly vigorous investigations of their agencies, they do less digging than they could and find out less than they should. Given their lack of legislative power, what these committees know or don't know may not matter much anyway. According to Dodd and Schott, it all adds up to the conclusion that "the GOC's simply have not proved to be aggressive oversight agents of Congress."[33]

Non-Committee Oversight

Though most oversight is conducted by committees, Congress can, and sometimes does, use its four major resource agencies to monitor bureaucratic performance. Of the four—the Congressional Research Service, the General Accounting Office, the Office of Technology Assessment, and the Congressional Budget Office —only the GAO has a long tradition of oversight responsibility, but all four can be used for different aspects of the oversight business.

The Congressional Research Service (formerly the Legislative Reference Service) has been providing information to members of Congress for most of this century. The 1970's saw CRS increase dramatically in terms of staff size and budget as it took on new responsibilities assigned to it in the Legislative Reorganization Act of 1970. These new responsibilities included some oversight-related activities, and, while it may be a bit early to draw any firm conclusions about its effectiveness as an oversight agency, Dodd and Schott have observed that, during the subsequent decade, "CRS . . . moved somewhat gingerly toward program evaluation and examination of individual agencies. Such reports, however, are rare and represent only a small fraction of its broad range of services. . . . Few if any [agency officials] to whom we talked felt that the work of the CRS contributed substantially to congressional oversight of their agencies or programs."[34]

The Office of Technology Assessment has been in existence for only a little over a decade and with an ambiguous legislative mandate and a staff of only forty professionals it has not really had much of a chance to become a significant oversight agency.[35] It has conducted (or contracted) major studies in several important policy areas, but some members have begun to use it to process constituent inquiries on science- and technology-related questions, and even leaving those aside, OTA receives far more requests than it can possibly handle.[36] In such a context, OTA can make only a very limited contribution to congressional oversight of administration.

The Congressional Budget Office is an even younger organization than the Office of Technology Assessment. CBO, and its first Director, Dr. Alice Rivlin, made a few headlines, but most of those were generated as a result of the exercise of the agency's responsibility for providing Congress with independent (non-OMB produced) economic forecasts and revenue and expenditure projections. Direct contacts between CBO and agency personnel are on the rise and this creates a definite potential for greater congressional access to information about agency performance. The fact that this information enters the Congress through the two Budget Committees or the House or Senate leadership, groups not tied directly to either the authorization or appropriations subsystems, may one day significantly change the nature of congressional oversight. At this point, however, most students of the CBO would agree with Dodd and Schott that "few observers either on the Hill or in the agencies suggest that the congressional budget process has led directly to more intensive and enduring oversight."[37]

This brings us to the federal government's chief auditor, the General Accounting Office. Created in 1921 with financial oversight as one of its key objectives, the GAO has become the Congress's most important and effective non-committee overseer of bureaucracy. A GAO audit is far more than a "look at the agency's books." In the words of one well-known student of General Accounting Office operations, its activities include "checking for compliance with applicable laws and regulations; examining the efficiency and economy of operations; and reviewing the results of operations to evaluate whether the desired results, including legislatively prescribed objectives, have been effectively achieved." [38] A tall order, but a professional staff of over 3,800 is attempting to fill it, and when they do, oversight is a likely by-product.

Significant as its contributions to congressional oversight of administration can be, there are limitations on the GAO's oversight role. One important limitation is self-imposed. During the early 1970's, the Congress became more and more interested in program evaluation and attempted to get the GAO to take the lead in conducting such evaluations throughout the federal bureaucracy. The Comptroller General, fearing that such responsibility would outstrip the agency's capacity to handle it and would detract from the performance of its traditional financial responsibilities, resisted these efforts.[39] Backed up by the powerful Appropriations Committees, he succeeded in his resistance. A second limitation on GAO's oversight effectiveness is the result of the congressional convention that GAO reports are confidential until released by the member or committee that requested it.[40] This, of course, makes it possible for an authorization committee to bury a report critical of one of "its" agencies, thereby blunting GAO oversight of that particular bureaucratic subunit. Third, there appears to be a very close working relationship between the GAO and the Appropriations Committees, a relationship that may bring agency staff into the vortex of appropriations politics.[41] Finally, Congress has assigned a number of new responsibilities to the GAO in recent years, and it is likely that some of these have deflected the agency's attention from oversight-oriented tasks.

The GAO is clearly the best equipped of the four support agencies to perform the task of oversight, and there is evidence that it has done so. But there are serious constraints on even the GAO's ability to conduct oversight on behalf of Congress, and it

seems reasonable to conclude that non-committee-based oversight produces only a very limited amount of useful information
about agency activities.

Oversight Reviewed

Some people would argue that Congress knows less about bureaucracy than it could, others that it knows less than it should.
Both charges may be true. Still, this much is clear. Lots of information about bureaucratic performance does find its way to
the Congress. It comes in angry letters from constituents and
visits from lobbyists. It comes in sworn testimony and fat reports.
Mostly it comes in informal communications among compatriots.
But it comes. The bulk of it comes to authorization committees
and subcommittees and it is they who are almost always the ones
who will decide whether or not to share it and, more to the point,
whether or not to use it.

The Means of Congressional Influence

Congressional committees and subcommittees have generally
established close and cooperative working relationships with the
agencies they find within their respective policy orbits. As a result, they can exercise a good bit of influence informally. Indeed,
much of the influence Congress exercises over bureaucratic decision making is not influence in the sense of one side dictating to
another or convincing the other to change its mind, but more
like the sort of cooperative give and take one finds among partners convinced that they can/must/should work together.

Cooperation, good will, and informal contact may abound,
but Congress does have formal powers it can and does use to
influence bureaucracy and they are important. They are important in part because agency-subcommittee relationships are not
eternally harmonious. Subcommittees sometimes have to "get

tough" with their agencies. They are also important because, as Dodd and Schott are careful to point out, Congress's informal influence over bureaucracy depends heavily for its success on the existence of its formal controls. Creating agencies, assigning programs, approving top-level appointments, writing budgets and spending instructions, but, most of all, passing laws, Congress has its opportunities to push most agencies toward the straight and narrow.

Legislation

The power to pass laws lies at the heart of all of Congress's influence over bureaucracy. Most agencies came into existence when Congress passed a law. They have programs to carry out because Congress passed laws assigning those programs, and, most of the time, they have the money to do their jobs because Congress passed a law giving it to them. New laws could move their programs, reduce their authority, or even put them out of business. The use of the power to write laws to shape bureaucratic structure and determine the budget will be discussed in succeeding sections. In this section I want to deal only with the initial grant of authority, the basic agency charter.

Every agency has some sort of basic charter. Somewhere there is a law—for some agencies there are several—that gives some idea of why an agency exists, what it is supposed to try to accomplish, and the means that will be at its disposal. All of these can be important ingredients in an agency's style, approach, and policies. The United States Fish and Wildlife Service was created "to conserve, protect, and enhance fish and wildlife and their habitats for the continuing benefit of the American people." [42] It is expected to provide leadership and empowered to conduct research that includes "surveillance of pesticides, heavy metals, and thermal pollution." [43] But it cannot cite a paper mill for putting chemicals in a river, take a nuclear power plant to court because the lake is getting too warm, or ban 2,4,5,T because the birds are dying. Only other agencies can do those things. As noted in the previous chapter, the Bureau of Mines was probably never all that dedicated to the idea of vigorous enforcement of mine safety legislation, but operating with authority to say "That's not a nice thing to do!" or "We hereby order you to close this mine," and nothing in between, made it pretty tough for that particular agency to move very far toward its legislatively prescribed goals. An agency's basic charter really is crucial.

Eventually that charter has to pass muster with the whole Congress, but in all but a handful of cases, the really significant tests come at the subcommittee and then the full committee level. Failure there is failure. Success there does not guarantee success on the floor, but most of the time betting against a positive committee recommendation is a lot like betting that the Yankees did not win the pennant in 195–. Your chances are 2 in 10. (For the Yankees, 1954 and 1959.)

Formal rules that make it virtually impossible for a bill to reach the floor of the House without committee approval take the place of central clearance and the veto, but the result is the same. If an agency wants authority its committee doesn't feel it should have, that authority can easily be withheld. Senate committees can be by-passed a bit more easily, but it happens seldom enough that they, too, can expect to make a No stick.

The battered but still powerful norm of reciprocity gives committees something that the President seldom has. The committee can not only block what it doesn't like, but can pass a good bit of what it does. This can enhance a committee's influence over agency policy making in one or more of three interrelated ways. First, if the committee wants an agency to move in a certain direction, it can probably get that agency the authority to act. The agency may not act anyway, but there is a good chance that it will. Second, if a committee is unhappy with the way in which an agency is using authority it currently has, the committee can take the lead in trying to pull that authority away. This is precisely what happened to the Federal Trade Commission in 1965 when the two Commerce Committees led the congressional charge against proposed FTC regulation of cigarette advertising.[44] When the dust had settled, the FTC was forbidden from any effort to require health warnings in any tobacco industry advertising. Finally, committees are in a far better bargaining position vis-à-vis the agencies than is the President. The Chief can punish, but rarely reward. The committee can do both. It can say "We'll stop it" and deliver, but it can also say, "We'll get it" and stand a pretty good chance of being true to its word then as well. This has to increase an agency's incentive to listen.

Most of what Congress can do to, or for, executive branch agencies it does by passing laws. At the core of all of these laws is a basic charter that tries to spell out what difference a particular agency is supposed to make in the world and the tools it will be given to try to make that difference. These things matter deeply to bureaucrats. They have to live within them and they try to live up to them. The authorizing committees and subcommittees of the two houses of Congress have a tremendous amount of influence over these basic charters and through that influence a substantial impact on agency policy making. Some of it is direct—agencies do a lot of what they are told they should do and very little of what they are told they shouldn't—and some of it is indirect—with that kind of influence over questions of such importance comes considerable bargaining power—but direct or indirect there is enough of it to conclude that passing laws gives congressional committees a lot of say over what happens at most executive branch agencies.

Structure

As noted in the previous chapter, the creation/abolition of agencies, location of authority, and assignment of programs to specific bureaucratic subunits are structural questions with significant policy implications. There are other such questions as well, and there is even an informal side to the issue of bureaucratic structure; that is, the balance of power between agency careerists and their departmental superiors can be affected by things never written down or passed into law.

Members of Congress are acutely aware that designing the bureaucratic structure is a high-stakes game. Consider this colorful lament by Montana Senator Burton Wheeler as he bitterly opposed the first effort to grant reorganization authority to the President: "So who is going to do it? Some professor or some clerk in the department is going to do it. They are going to be the boys who will do the work and they are going to say to my people in Montana, 'we are going to abolish the Bureau of Indian Affairs' . . . although they have never set foot on an Indian reservation in their lives and have never seen an Indian, except in the moving picture in New York City, they are going to sit down in some office in Washington, prepare reports and tell the members of the Senate and of the House what ought to be done." [45] The Senator's concern does not seem to be with questions of administrative neatness or proper theories of organization.

Members of Congress are not only aware of the stakes involved in structuring bureaucracy, they have a clear idea of the kind of structure they want to create and why. An executive branch composed of lots of narrowly focused agencies, each created by statute, possessing its own charter and the authority to act within its own sphere, and with program assignments fixed by law, will be highly responsive to the wishes of congressional subcommittees, enhancing the power of these legislative subunits and, ultimately, of the individual members themselves. In the first place, such a structure keeps power and authority away from the political executives who operate at the upper levels of the various departments. Agencies that are created by law, are assigned programs by law, and have the authority to act on their own can resist an awful lot of pressure from the top. By denying the political executives their number one resource—legal authority over agencies—Congress weakens their hand considerably. Second, the policy specialists who control these semi-autonomous agencies are highly responsive to subcommittee sentiment. They know that what the subcommittee gave the agency—authority, programs, life itself—it could probably take away, and in any event, as noted time and time again, the two sides are drawn together by common background, shared knowledge, and concern for the interests of the same people. The more power, authority, and program responsibility can be kept at the agency level, the more influence subcommittees can have over its use, and that is precisely what the Congress has chosen to do.

As noted earlier, the bulk of congressional influence over executive branch structure is exercised by passing laws. Of the eight operating bureaus in the Department of Interior, seven were created by statute.[46] The remaining one, the Bureau of Land Management, did come into existence as a result of a presidential reorganization plan, but the plan simply merged two existing Interior Department bureaus—the General Land Office and the Grazing Service—and it occurred in 1946, when such authority came with far fewer restrictions on its use. In any event, one doubts that BLM autonomy has suffered drastically from the circumstances of its creation. Program assignments, too, are fixed by statute, though here arguments over which agency should administer a particular program are just as likely to be showdowns pitting one congressional subcommittee against another as they are subcommittee versus the President or his departmental representatives.[47] Finally, Congress prefers to place authority in the hands of program or agency administrators rather than those of their departmental superiors. The body has budged on this occasionally of late—the Interior Secretary has a good bit of formal authority over resource use policy in the West—but Congress watches the exercise of that authority carefully and has used its law-making power to limit how the Secretary could use it when the members did not like what they saw. That seldom happens to a bureau chief.

For most of the past half-century, Congress has agreed to share control over bureaucratic structure with the President. The Chief was permitted to propose changes in the shape of the executive branch, but as the years went on the restrictions on what he could even propose grew tighter and tighter—by the 1970's he could not submit any reorganization plan that substantially restructured any of the independent regulatory commissions, created a new Cabinet department, or proposed the elimination of any agency or program created by statute — and Congress insisted on saving the final word for itself. That word was sometimes Yes — we got HEW, the Environmental Protection Agency, the Drug Enforcement Administration, and, as noted a moment ago, the Bureau of Land Management this way — but it was just as likely to be No. John Kennedy was rebuffed in his effort to create a Department of Housing and Urban Affairs through such a plan, and every President from FDR through Jimmy Carter saw Congress turn down their best-laid plans.[48] The reasons nearly always revolved around the protection of subcommittee turf. Chet Holifield (D. Cal.), who chaired the House Government Operations Committee as it considered Richard Nixon's plans for a sweeping reorganization of the executive branch, turned out to be a pretty fair prophet when he said: "If by this reorganization you affect in a major way the powers of the various committees in the Congress, you may as well forget it. The only way I know to get one or more of these departments through is to allow the committees that now have the programs within their jurisdictions to follow their programs, just as they are followed now, and authorize these programs wherever they are distributed."[49] The plan never got out of the House Rules Committee, and most of the blame or credit belongs to the Chairs of the various authorizing committees.[50]

It is hard to say if Congress will restore the President's reorganization authority. With the status of the congressional veto extremely cloudy — one house vetoes are out, but two house by concurrent resolution may be OK — I doubt he will get it back in the near future. From the congressional perspective, there is too much at stake not to have the last word and, so long as the President must make all of his restructuring moves through specific legislation, Congress retains that word.

Finally, members of Congress work toward their goal of an executive branch of autonomous subunits informally. They do so by providing political support for agencies in trouble, and, as Harold Seidman notes, that support "is quickly forthcoming when they need help in blunting or negating Presidential directives which they oppose or in chasing poachers from their domains." [51] It is difficult to see this sort of informal political support in action—Presidents and Cabinet Secretaries rarely issue press releases detailing the nature of the battle or the terms of their surrender—but nearly all observers of American politics agree that such congressional support is common and that it constitutes a major weapon for agency careerists as they struggle with their department superiors for control over policy decisions.

Members of Congress firmly believe that agency autonomy will serve their political and policy interests. They use the power to legislate to provide important formal protections for that autonomy in the form of guaranteed existence, independent statutory authority and program assignments fixed in the law, and their political power to supplement these formal guarantees with equally important informal ones. The result is a fragmented executive branch far more responsive to the Congress than to the man in the White House.

Personnel Selection

Even though a lot of us who know better refer to them as presidential appointees, the Congress has a significant say in the question of who will occupy the 2,500 or so positions at the top of the bureaucratic pyramid. Formally, of course, the Senate possesses the constitutional authority to confirm presidential nominations for these top-level jobs. Informally, the upper house has taken that magnificent constitutional phrase "by and with the advice and consent" to heart, offering the Chief Executive plenty of the former as he contemplates his choices. The House has no official role in this personnel selection process, but that has certainly not prevented individual House members from making their preferences known. Both houses prefer a clientele-oriented appointment pattern and use the constitutional authority of the Senate and the informal influence of the Senate and the House to guarantee it.

Once the President submits a nomination for a top-level bureaucratic post, that nomination is submitted to a Senate committee, namely, to the legislative committee with jurisdiction over the department the individual will enter. There have been some internal squabbles, especially right after major committee reorganizations, but, for the most part, there is agreement about which committees confirm which bureaucrats. Committees have wide latitude as they play their part in the confirmation process. They may take a couple of months, conducting a careful background check, exhaustive hearings, and closed sessions with spirited internal debate. Or they may take a couple of weeks with a few ritual questions about financial holdings and/or statements about the glories of economical and efficient government.

Because the Agriculture Committee reviews all of the nominations for jobs at the top of the Agriculture Department, we can be certain that the affected farm producer groups will be offered the opportunity to express their preferences on these nominations, and those preferences will be taken seriously. Business leaders will be accorded the same opportunity to comment on Commerce Department nominees, Western land users (and sometimes environmentalists) on the Interior Department names, and so on. At the committee stage of the process there is plenty of room for clientele and professional input and influence.

Committee recommendations are generally accepted on the Senate floor. This is particularly true for the less visible subcabinet posts. Here the committee decision is almost certain to be ratified, often by voice vote of the handful of Senators who bothered to attend that particular session. Even the major Cabinet positions tend to be thought of as committee preserves, and an Armed Services Committee recommendation on a nominee for Secretary of Defense or a Foreign Relations Committee decision on a Secretary of State is almost certain to stick. Whatever clientele influence has been felt at the committee level is quite unlikely to be countered on the Senate floor.

In the end, the Senate consents to the overwhelming majority of the President's nominations. The exceptions make headlines. Jimmy Carter's nomination of Ted Sorenson for CIA Director, Ronald Reagan's choice of Ernest LeFevre for the State Department's top human rights post, and Richard Nixon's nomination of John Knowles for the number one health job at HEW, all had to be withdrawn amid great presidential embarrassment, and Harry Truman's showdown with Lyndon Johnson over Truman's effort to retain Leland Olds on the old Federal Power Commission was livelier than you would expect, even from battlers of their stature.[52] Entertaining as they may be, however, they are exceptions. Once it reaches this stage, Presidents get pretty much what they ask for.

This comes as no surprise, of course, since, as we saw in the previous chapter, Presidents are extremely careful about what they ask for. Knowing that their nominees must survive the test of Senate confirmation, and that the committees at the center of the process have strong clientele interests to protect, Presidents quickly come to the conclusion that a clientele-oriented pattern of nominations is a political must. Such a pattern has its philosophical and technological justification as well—these groups deserve representation in bureaucracy and can be a source, often the only real source, of people with the experience and expertise to run the various departments—but the test of Senate confirmation is never far from the President's mind, and whatever political mileage there is in Cabinet and sub-Cabinet appointments is found among clientele groups, not the general public. Every President soon learns that the easiest way to be certain that a nomination will be acceptable to the Senate is to ask beforehand. The leader of the President's party, key members of the relevant committee, and possibly a few other Senators will be asked about a particular individual or set of individuals. They may be invited to add names to the White House list or, even more likely, to take names off that list. Major clientele groups will get the same opportunities. In effect, for most top-level bureaucratic positions, the formal confirmation process is a reconfirmation of an individual deemed acceptable to all of the "relevant" parties in an informal process already complete.

It is primarily through this informal process that the Senate manages to guarantee that clientele interests will be well represented in the upper echelons of the federal bureaucracy, though no one, least of all the Senators, ought to forget that the influence of the Senate's "advice" derives from the need for its "consent." Applying as their main standard the acceptability of the nominee to the clientele groups of the agencies that constitute a particular department, Senators offer their advice and exercise considerable influence over the creation of the list of names they will soon be asked to confirm. The result is a set of top-level departmental officials sympathetic to the clientele groups of their respective departments and to the agency-committee alliances that represent those groups inside the government. This is not a group of men and women ready to launch a serious challenge to the agencies and their narrow view of the public interest.

The Budget

As noted in the previous chapter, the budget-making process is in a rather chaotic state. Indeed, one suspects that, at least among those old enough to have experienced them, there is a certain nostalgia for the good old days when House Appropriations Subcommittees held exhaustive (and exhausting) hearings and made recommendations that had a better than 80 percent chance of passing intact on the House floor, when the Senate Committee served as appeals court for angry agencies and their supporters, and all executive branch careerists agreed with the colleague who told Aaron Wildavsky that the House Appropriations Subcommittees "can do you a world of good and they can cut your throat." [53] Off-budget and backdoor spending, Budget Resolutions I and II, reconciliation and paying the bills by continuing resolution have altered all of that, perhaps for good.

Still, Congress is not all the way out of the budget business, at least not as far as most agencies are concerned. In the first place, Congress is in a far better position than the President to deal with agencies engaged in off-budget or backdoor spending since the authority to guarantee loans and so forth that makes up much of such spending came from Congress in the first place and it can more easily act to pull it back. This is not to say the job is easy for the legislative branch—just easier than for the Chief. More to the point, agencies still funded primarily through the annual appropriations process must face the same sort of hearings they faced twenty years ago. Appropriations Subcommittee batting averages may have dropped a bit in the recent past, but the fact that the bureau chiefs studied by Herbert Kaufman engaged in the most intensive preparation of the year when going over to face those very subcommittees suggests that career bureaucrats still respect the Congress's power over the federal budget.[54] Finally, Congress has turned more and more to the use of a key fiscal oversight technique, the issuing of detailed spending instructions. Michael Kirst found that, as far back as the late 1960's, appropriations bills generally contained five formal statutory restrictions on agency spending and the reports accompanying each appropriations act were likely to contain thirty or more informal provisions relating to the use of the dollars appropriated.[55] Despite some strong criticism of the process by congressional leaders, it is alive and well as illustrated by the fact that the Food and Drug Administration was instructed in both 1979 and 1980 "not to promulgate regulations prohibiting the addition of antibiotics to animal feed."[56] A frustrated FDA went along with the instructions.[57]

The days when the mere mention of a House Appropriations Subcommittee Chair's name could cause an agency head to turn pale and reach for his ulcer medication are likely gone, never to be seen again. But congressional influence over agency budgets has not disappeared. Subcommittee hearings are still a command performance and agency directors know they had better be good. An awful lot of agencies still run most of their operations on appropriated dollars and an angry subcommittee will get even sooner or later. Finally come the spending instructions. Increasingly specific and occasionally quite unrelated to spending itself —the House once passed such an appropriations rider instructing the Departments of Labor and Health and Human Services not to issue "any rules containing hiring, promotion, or admissions quotas based on race, creed, color or sex" [58]—these instructions do more than merely flex a bit of congressional muscle. They affect policy. When Kirst asked agency officials about these restrictions in 1968 they said, "We just have to live with them." [59] If the FDA action noted earlier is any guide, they still do. In fact, these spending instructions may offer the opportunity to deal with agencies whose off-budget spending irks the Congress. After all, if an appropriations rider not to issue rules prohibiting antibiotics in animal feed will stick, why not one to prohibit certain kinds of loans from being guaranteed? It may not be the halcyon days of Congressman John Rooney, but reports of the death of congressional use of budgetary authority to influence bureaucratic policy making are greatly exaggerated.

Congressional Staff: A Note of Caution

Throughout this chapter I have used the phrase "members and staff" as if it were Amos 'n Andy or Ozzie and Harriet. There are more than a few people who think of members and staff as more like Taylor and Burton, or at least Simon and Garfunkel. Counting committees, subcommittees, caucuses, and individual member offices, there are nearly 1,000 separate congressional entities that employ close to 20,000 people in staff positions. [60] In that kind of context, we can hardly expect all of the actions taken by staff people to be consistent with the desires of the members or subcommittees that employ them. So it is possible that some of the influence that subcommittees have over agency decision making is exercised by staffers acting on their own with no particular knowledge of, or concern for, the wishes of subcommittee members. It is possible, but not very likely. Despite a situation almost designed for administrative chaos, I am convinced that congressional staff, particularly subcommittee staff, fit into the cooperative agency-committee relationship so neatly that "members and staff" really is far closer to Ozzie and Harriet than Dick and Liz.

In the first place, every staffer has direct and powerful ties to some member or members. Loyalty is expected—by both sides—and it is almost always forthcoming. The loyalty of personal staffs is just that, personal. Despite repeated warnings from party leaders about the dangers of an inexperienced staff, new House members tend to fill three out of four personal staff slots with newcomers to Capitol Hill.[61] Nearly all of them go way back with that particular member. On the darker side, staffers have no form of job security other than continued loyalty from the boss. One measure of the closeness of the member-staff relationship can be seen in the startling fact that nearly 75 percent of personal staffers leave congressional employ when the member they worked for moves on.

Committee and subcommittee staff operate in a somewhat different environment, but Salisbury and Shepsle find an emerging consensus among students of congressional staffs that "the overwhelming number of staffers in every nominal category are tied to a principal or patron."[62] It is true that a high percentage of these subcommittee employees stick around even when the full committee or their own subcommittee chairmanship changes hands, but Salisbury and Shepsle offer the intriguing speculation that the desire to survive such leadership changes may make these men and women even more loyal to their bosses. How better to show other senior members of the committee that a staffer can be trusted? Remember, one of these senior members will be the next Chair.[63]

Loyalty of this sort doesn't put the staff member in a straightjacket. He or she still has some room for independent judgment.

But there isn't all that much room nor all that much desire to use or expand it. Ties before either came to Congress, years together, a mutual weeding-out process that eliminates staffers with the desire for a lot of independence, and the knowledge of every staff person on the Hill that the boss can show him or her the door anytime should be enough to keep most of these thousands of employees in line with their bosses' preferences.

Ironically, the second force that keeps congressional staff people close to the members they serve and makes them eager participants in the cooperative agency-subcommittee relationship is their own ambition. Some staffers are politically ambitious, and a good many of those eventually end up winning congressional seats of their own after a period of staff service. Even more common is the desire to "go downtown," that is, to find a job in the executive branch. For those with five to ten years of experience it may be a middle-level policy or management position, for those who have put in their twenty it could be a Supergrade or even a political appointment at the Assistant Secretary level. Who better to hire for a congressional liaison position than someone who survived two decades on the Hill and knows everyone on the committees that affect a particular agency or cluster of agencies? Finally, for a growing number of staff people, there is the possibility of a spot with one of the many professional groups, trade associations, or specialized law offices or lobbying firms that make up one of Washington's major growth industries. All of these groups need contacts and access—that's mostly what they sell, after all—and staffers who leave, especially those who leave the right committees, generally have plenty of both.

Whether the goal is a GS-15 slot at the Bureau of Land Management, a job as Vice-President for Governmental Affairs with the National Association of Wheat Growers, or a chance to run for the House seat in Iowa's 5th District, the staff member about to make the break is going to need two things, strong support from his or her congressional patron and a good reputation amongst those who control the distribution of jobs in this particular policy area. The absence of either one could prove fatal.

Departing staffers headed for the so-called "K Street Corridor" of law offices and lobbying firms probably have the most obvious need for a glowing recommendation from some member or members of Congress. As noted a moment ago, they are being hired because they are known and respected on the Hill. They can get into the right rooms and offices at the right times. Support from the right members is the credential that verifies their claim. They cannot afford to jeopardize it. Those who hope to head for an appointed job or congressional liaison spot are in precisely the same position for precisely the same reasons. Those who hope to land career spots may be a little less vulnerable, but unless they have outstanding credentials as a policy specialist, their edge on the competition has to come from the fact that they are well liked on the Hill. So they had better stay that way. Even those who expect to run for seats of their own may need their patron's support —especially if the plan is to try for that patron's seat upon his or her retirement. If the staffer wins, good relations with other members wouldn't hurt an incoming freshman either. In short, if a staff member wants to go anywhere else in government or in the government-influencing business, it is best to stay on good terms with the members he or she is called upon to serve. Keeping the staffer's actions as close as possible to the members' preferences is essential if the relationship between the two is going to thrive.

Ambition also induces staff people, especially committee and subcommittee staff, to fit themselves into the cooperative atmosphere of most agency-subcommittee relationships. Any staffer who has generated ill will between a subcommittee and one or more of its agencies is hardly going to be welcomed with open arms by those agencies when he or she comes knocking on the door looking for employment. Nor is that staff person going to be particularly well received at a trade association that has to work with both agency and subcommittee. Safer candidates are bound to be available somewhere. So for anyone with plans to leave a congressional staff position for the bureaucracy or a high-paying lobbying job, keeping agency-subcommittee relationships close and cooperative can pay big dividends.

Ambition, like loyalty, leaves some room for independence. Staff people can, and no doubt sometimes do, act on their own. But if a staff member does want to run for office, get a job in the federal bureaucracy, or latch onto a lobbying spot, he or she has to be liked, respected, and trusted by the members with (for) whom he or she has worked. The safest route to that destination is to stick as close as possible to what the staffer knows is acceptable to that member or members.

The very existence of nearly 1,000 subunits employing upwards of 20,000 people has all the earmarks of an administrative nightmare. There can be no doubt in anyone's mind that parts of that nightmare come true every day. Still, I am convinced that loyalty to the people they work for and their own ambitions keep most staff members on a fairly narrow path and, more to the point, that that path makes committee and subcommittee staff willing and active partners in the durable agency-subcommittee alliances that are the major vehicle for congressional influence over the federal bureaucracy. To disrupt those alliances would be to court disaster, a disaster that could cut off all sorts of avenues to a golden future even as it creates an uncomfortable present. It is hard to imagine why anyone, especially anyone who had survived in a staff role for more than a couple of years, would run such a risk.

Summary and Conclusion

Congress has a great deal to say about what happens in the federal bureaucracy. Indeed, in summing up his two years of observing the activities of a half-dozen bureau chiefs, Herbert Kaufman concluded that *"no other external group or institution enjoyed quite so commanding a position as Congress."* [64] It occupies that position because it has precisely what the President lacks, a cooperative relationship with agency careerists that makes these policy specialists willing to listen, a fairly steady flow of information about what most agencies are up to, and the tools to do every agency plenty of good — or harm — should the Congress feel the need.

Where the President, perceived as a short-term amateur, meets a stone wall of resistance from the policy specialists that dominate agency decision making, congressional committees and subcommittees find these very same men and women willing to enter into a policy-making partnership. Each side has a great deal to gain from such a partnership, of course, since the agency staff can get the kind of political support that is vital to their success plus the legitimacy that makes them acceptable policy makers in a democratic system and subcommittee members and staff can advance important personal (re-election or a good job downtown) and policy goals. Together they can do a whole lot more than they could possibly do apart. Besides that, there is a certain natural affinity between the two sides that is supplemented by years of working together and continued concentration on a fairly narrow range of issues, issues that have both personal and political interest to both sides. In this sort of context, anything other than cooperation would be a real mystery.

While the President spends his time wondering — or, more likely not even bothering to wonder — what most agencies are doing, congressional committees and subcommittees are busy finding out. Congress certainly doesn't know everything going on at every agency. How could it when most agencies don't know everything going on within their own hallways? But Congress hears a great deal, much of it given over quite voluntarily, and it is much better equipped to make use of what it hears than the President can ever be. The odds that any agency will be out of step with the wishes of its subcommittees for any length of time without being discovered are pretty slim. This, in turn, provides another incentive to cooperation and enhances congressional influence over bureaucratic decision making.

Finally, when an angry President reaches into the closet for a club to use to beat bureaucracy back into line, he finds a pretty small stick. When Congress reaches in it comes out with a war club suitable for the task. Despite the fact that the President has a share in answering all of these questions, Congress has managed to reserve for itself the final say on which agencies live and which die, on what sort of departmental home they will have, and on which programs they will administer, what legal authority they will have to administer them with, and how much money they can spend as they do it. No agency could ignore that sort of power, even if it wanted to, of course, so we have one more strong inducement for agency careerists to work closely with their subcommittees. The penalty for not doing so could be severe.

I have probably left the impression that agency-subcommittee relationships take place in some sort of Camelot where no agency head has ever been angered by congressional interference and no subcommittee Chair ever frustrated by bureaucratic intransigence. Such is obviously not the case. Agencies do sometimes chafe under the congressional bridle, and just as they have been known to use subcommittee instructions to frustrate presidential efforts at control, they have occasionally responded to subcommittee suggestions with "The Secretary (President) has ordered us not to do that." Even more common are efforts to exploit the ever-present tension between authorizing and appropriating subcommittees, or the occasional struggles between legislative subcommittees competing for control over a particular policy area, by playing one subcommittee off against the other. In the long run, it may indeed be impossible to serve two masters, but, for the moment, if you can get them arguing with one another you may be able to ignore both and do what you wish. Finally, an agency may just dig in its heels and tell a subcommittee No. Agencies are less prone to resist the subcommittee than the President, since resisting the former strains an important long-term relationship and has a lower probability of success, but if a particular agency feels the stakes in a specific decision are high enough, it may run the risk.

Congress doesn't always win any more than the President always loses. Still, agency-subcommittee cooperation is the norm, agency-subcommittee conflict the exception. There is far more to unite than to divide them and they know it. Both sides will give a little to avoid conflict when they can, and if a fight does erupt, they will make every effort to resolve it before outsiders become aware of it and try to intervene. Both sides are convinced that the benefits of long-term cooperation far outweigh those of even a victory in short-term conflict, and they act accordingly.

One question remains. What does Congress do with all of this influence? What interests does it choose to protect? What values does it hope to advance? As with the President, the answer is a matter of judgment, but I believe there is substantial evidence to show that the interests are those of the organized groups most directly involved in a particular policy area, the value, a kind of vulgarized version of an important democratic precept, responsiveness to minority concerns.

With committee and subcommittee assignments routinely handed out on the basis of constituent interests, interest group PAC's funneling money to men and women on the appropriate committees, and an atmosphere of mutual trust and cooperation generated by repeated interaction, it should come as no surprise that congressional committees and subcommittees use their influence with their agencies to protect the interests of the groups who bring them the votes, dollars, and information they so obviously need. An Agriculture Committee composed of farm district representatives, many of them raised on farms or in small towns in farming areas, drawing campaign financing from the American Farm Bureau Federation and the major commodity associations, and working day in and day out with representatives of these organizations, that decided *not* to protect the interests of agricultural producers would be a real man bites dog story. The dog would bite back. Since nearly all of the influence Congress exercises over the federal bureaucracy is exercised by subcommittees over the agencies in their area of responsibility, there can't be any doubt that congressional influence leads directly to interest group influence. There may be some counterbalance. Each chamber has been known to overrule its committees on occasion, but the occasions are anything but frequent. With only the rarest of exceptions, congressional power is committee and subcommittee power and that means interest group power.

Interest group power isn't all bad. Democracy does mean more than counting heads, after all. Imposing majority preferences on a group passionately opposed to those preferences can be dangerous, to the dissenting minority itself and, in the extreme case, to the very fabric of democracy.[65] What would happen if the Farmers Home Administration met its "legal" obligation and foreclosed on all 65,000 farms currently three years behind in mortgage payments to the agency? Beyond that, as Emmette Redford observed, "It is difference in quantity of interest that creates the toughest quandries in the application of democratic theory to specific policy issues. The opportunities of men are not usually determined by sweeping decisions equally applicable to all, but grow out of policies affecting particular groups of men selectively and differently. And when as a result unequal amounts of interest exist for different persons, . . . numbers alone may not determine the equities."[66] If protectionist legislation really worked (protected the jobs it is supposed to protect), would it really be fair to ask one man to give up his job so another could save $500 on the price of a car? Is there a magic formula that tells us how many $500's have to be saved before it becomes fair?

Interest group power is a way of trying to deal with the problems that could be caused by running roughshod over the deeply held feelings of a minority of the population or the high stakes interests of a few just to satisfy someone's notion of majority preferences. I believe there are sound reasons to conclude it is not a very good way, but this is not the place to consider those reasons.[67] Instead I will register only this objection. Congressional committees have become such effective servants of those interests, and the value of minority responsiveness they purport to represent, that they have lost sight of the underlying democratic commitment to majority interests. Numbers alone may not determine the equities, but they have to count for something.

So, in the end, Congress has a good bit of influence over bureaucratic decision making. That influence is in the hands of subcommittees with powerful ties to a very predictable set of organized interests. Some of the members of these subcommittees may feel a little squeamish about consistently representing only one narrow view of the public interest, but most believe they are helping to make a democratic system more responsive. It may be nothing more than a rationalization, but in the circles in which they travel, it's an easy one to sell.

Bureaucracy and the Public

4

Bureaucrats, like politicians and political scientists, know there is no such thing as the public. But there are people, and some of these people feel they ought to have some influence over bureaucratic policy making.

There is that ever elusive but always talked about "general public," and there are organizations that have assumed the name Public Interest Groups and claim to speak for that general public. There are clientele groups—organized interest groups served and/or regulated by a particular agency—and professional associations composed of people with the same subject matter expertise and commitments as those of an agency's staff. There are also individual policy experts from the ranks of former officials, academe, and the growing number of policy "think tanks." Finally, there are groups of policy specific watchdogs as well as individual citizens who almost seem to feel themselves called to criticize bureaucracy and bureaucrats.

It adds up to seven different sets of people, each with some sort of reasonable claim that they ought to exercise some influence over bureaucracy. Some actually do.

Bureaucrats and Their Supporters

Three sets of people seeking to influence bureaucratic decision making can be lumped together under the title bureaucratic supporters. Clientele groups, professional associations, and individual policy experts all hope to cultivate close and cooperative working relationships with the agencies that concern them. Once again, the irresistible combination of self-interest and empathy makes it happen.

Bureaucrats and Clientele Groups

Every agency does something to or for somebody. That's what agencies are for. Consequently, for every agency, there are groups of people that care very deeply about that agency's people, policies, and programs. Those that organize and try to influence "their" agencies are clientele groups. As was the case with congressional subcommittees, these clientele groups can supply an agency with power and legitimacy.

Clientele groups are an excellent agency power base for precisely the same reasons that subcommittees are. They are around for the long haul, they know the policy area, and they have political power. No one doubts the long-term nature of clientele group interest in agency policy making. As long as the decisions continue to affect the lives and interests of group members the group is going to be there. In addition, people directly affected by an agency's programs are bound to know something about those programs and the issues and problems that spawned them. Hospital administrators do know something about the hospital business — including something about how to organize and regulate it — timber companies know something about forest management, and farmers know something about agriculture. Most clientele groups maintain a permanent staff, with a high proportion of its membership drawn from the same professions as the staff of the agency itself. Indeed, Dennis Ippolito and Thomas

Walker contend that interest group representatives are generally among the most knowledgeable and respected participants at congressional committee hearings.[1] Finally, as we saw in the previous chapter, these clientele groups are almost always on friendly terms with the very subcommittees that have the greatest impact on "their" agencies.[2] These connections can be based directly on constituency concerns. House Agriculture, Merchant Marine and Fisheries, and Interior, for example, are heavily tipped toward the regions that are home to the industries those committees affect.[3] They can also be based on dollars; that is, there is lots of PAC money poured into congressional campaigns and it is targeted toward "candidates who occupy . . . position[s] of special relevance to the policy area of immediate concern to the interest group."[4] They can even be based on knowledge. Such groups really can be one more source of information for an information-starved Congress. Whatever its basis, bureaucrats know that their clientele groups have power where it counts.

Clientele groups also supply agencies with a further dose of legitimacy. Working with these groups is one way of working directly with the people. It is true that interest groups are not "the people," but they are people, people directly affected by agency policies and obviously concerned about what those policies will be. As we shall see later in this chapter, many of the forms of clientele participation in agency decision making are open, public, and on the record. So, even though clientele groups are the cursed "special interests," their active support for "their" agencies does provide further legitimacy to those agencies and their policies.

Clientele groups, too, benefit from close and cooperative working relationships with their agencies. Such groups quickly conclude that influence over policy implementation can bring substantial economic benefits. Timber companies that want to log the national forests must come to the Forest Service. Ranchers who want to graze cattle or sheep on publicly owned range land must go to the Bureau of Land Management, as must oilmen and mine owners who want the minerals under that land, developers who want to put dude ranches or ski resorts on it, or loggers who want to cut its timber. The list of groups whose economic success depends in substantial measure on bureaucratic decisions could be extended indefinitely, and it would run the socio-economic gamut from New York stock brokers to Minnesota soybean growers. All have concluded that the best way to protect those economic interests is through close and cooperative relationships with the agencies whose decisions affect them.

Empathy, too, plays an important role in agency-clientele relationships. As noted earlier, bureaucratic recruitment patterns often produce a professional staff that closely resembles its clientele groups in background and heritage. The result is a sort of natural affinity between the two. The bonds of shared expertise and lifetime commitment to a particular set of policy issues or questions will serve to strengthen the clientele-agency attachment born of common background when it is present, and may even substitute for it when it is not. As Francis Rourke put it, "In its most developed form the relationship . . . is so close that it is difficult to know where the group leaves off and the agency begins."[5]

Bureaucrats and Their Clients: Some Exceptions

Some agency-clientele relationships are considerably less than smooth and harmonious. These exceptions to the rule of clientele-agency cooperation are likely in one or the other of two sets of circumstances.

First of all, some agencies serve or regulate clients who can't provide them with political power or legitimacy since these clients have none to give. Professionals who operate in policy areas such as corrections, vocational rehabilitation, mental health, or welfare cannot look to prisoners or parolees, the physically handicapped, individuals suffering from mental illness, or welfare recipients for the kind of political or even emotional support that Department of Agriculture bureaucrats can expect from farmers, Interior Department personnel from Western land users, or Treasury Department people from the banking industry.

With the self-interest motive largely removed, agency-clientele relationships would have to rest on empathy, and for most of these agencies, that basis, too, is missing. Most high-level corrections professionals have not done "hard time," nor are most welfare bureaucrats a year or two removed from the AFDC rolls. It does happen, but it is not the norm. Most of the men and women who occupy the key professional positions in these policy areas do have a great deal of sympathy for their clients, but sympathy is very different from empathy and a relationship based on the former will never have the closeness and the stability of one based on the latter.

With little for the agency to gain, and no feeling that "we" and "they" are really just a bigger "we," agency-clientele relationships will almost certainly become distant and strained. One frequent consequence of such a situation is even closer and more cooperative relations between agencies and their supporters in the community of experts in their particular policy area. Support from someone on the outside is vital for both power and legitimacy, and if it cannot come from clients, professional associations and individual policy experts are just about the only ones out there who can or will provide it. Welfare bureaucracies may keep considerable distance between themselves and the National Welfare Rights Organization, but to do so they must be that much closer to the National Association of Social Workers and the major graduate schools of social work. They are.

Not all of the agency-clientele relationships that deviate from the norm of partnership are found among agencies called upon to serve some of society's "losers." An agency can also get into that spot regulating some of society's "winners." The Federal Trade Commission has no support at all among used car dealers, funeral home directors, or the executives of Sears Roebuck, and the Occupational Safety and Health Administration has been forced to battle all the way to the Supreme Court to defend itself against textile and oil industry charges of arbitrary and capricious decision making.[6]

Not all regulator-regulated relationships are characterized by such rancor, of course. For most of its history, the Civil Aeronautics Board operated in close concert with the large commercial airlines,[7] and the old regional rate bureaus used by the Interstate Commerce Commission to screen and recommend on proposed freight rates virtually made the regulated into the regulators.[8] Close cooperation between regulatory commissions and the industries they regulated was so much the norm in the mid-1950's that Marver Bernstein argued that the commissions had been "captured" by the regulated businesses and that such capture was a natural stage in the life cycle of these commissions.[9] Two of the most frequently mourned captive commissions—the CAB and the ICC—have been "liberated" by legislation deregulating the airline and trucking industries, and there is reason to wonder how many commissions remain captives of their respective industries. Still, the Securities and Exchange Commission is awfully friendly to the major firms holding seats on the New York Stock Exchange, and the Nuclear Regulatory Commission has managed to delay, suspend, rewrite, or just plain ignore many of the safety regulations the commission itself produced in the wake of Three Mile Island.

It is clear now that relations between government regulators and the folks who must march to their rulebooks can vary from the sparks that flew between OSHA and the textile industry over cotton dust rules to the cozy accommodation over routes and rates that finally led California Representative John Moss to sue the CAB to force it to consider the interests of someone other than the airlines.[10] There are lots of spots in between and there is almost certainly a regulator-regulated relationship on each one. But how do we explain the variation? Why do some regulators end up in cooperation, almost collusion, with those they regulate while others keep a substantial distance from those who must comply with the rules and regulations they produce?

If we take Marver Bernstein's idea of capture as part of the life cycle of regulatory agencies literally, we would assume that age would play a role in generating these differences. By the time Bernstein wrote, the railroads had had three quarters of a century to capture the ICC and even the truckers had had the benefit of nearly thirty years to design and carry out a takeover strategy. In addition, the argument that organizations pursue their goals more vigorously when both the organization and its purposes are young is certainly plausible. OSHA and the EPA are just kids. Maybe they'll grow up.

The aging of a regulatory agency may have some impact on its relationship with those it must regulate, but age alone can hardly begin to explain the variation in the closeness (coolness) of regulator-regulated relations. After all, the FTC has been around a fairly long time and was over half a century old when it took some of the actions most offensive to those it regulates, and the CAB was devotedly serving airline interests by the time it was four. In fact, the only sustained period of "anti-airline" activity by the CAB came between 1974 and 1978 and followed thirty-five years of pro-industry policy.[11]

In the concluding chapter of his excellent collection *The Politics of Regulation*, James Q. Wilson provides some very solid leads for unraveling the mystery of regulator-regulated relations.[12] Extrapolating a bit from Wilson, we would expect to find the closest and most cooperative relationships between regulator and regulated in those situations in which it is a single industry that is to be regulated, the regulation is strictly economic (prices, types of services, etc.), the mandate includes or at least implies promotion of the health of the industry as well as regulation, and there is no clear or well-developed profession(s) devoted to this particular type of regulation. At the opposite end of the spectrum, we would expect coolness, distance, even hostility when an agency must regulate a number of industries—perhaps Industry itself—the regulation includes elements of health and/or safety, promotion is out of the picture (since the regulation is non-economic, this is pretty much automatic), and the regulators compose (are composed of) a clearly defined and self-conscious profession. As usual, there are all sorts of gray areas in between, but let's deal with the opposing archetypes and that should help to clarify what lies in between.

As Louis Kohlmeier pointed out years ago, regulatory bodies charged with both the regulation and the promotion of a specific industry are faced with a frustrating ambiguity.[13] On the one hand, they are expected to protect the public from poor service at unfair prices and, on the other, to get or keep an industry on its economic feet. It is ever so easy for regulators to begin to identify the health of the industry with that of the specific firms within that industry—what is the airline industry if not United, American, and TWA—and from there it is a short step to a variety of pro-industry policy choices. Add to this the fact that the regulation covers a single industry—meaning that daily contacts between regulator and regulated involve a very narrow set of people —and some sort of personal accommodation is almost inevitable. Because the regulation is exclusively economic, a regulator can easily avoid the cancer syndrome; that is, the worst that can happen from a regulator's decision is a transfer of income from one set of people to another. No one is going to die. Besides, the regulator knows the people who will be on the receiving end of the transfer, not those who will do the giving. Finally, in a good many situations, the regulators are not part of any clearly identifiable professional group devoted to the pursuit of the perfect regulatory policy for industry X. This is important in two ways. First, it means that there is no set of professional norms to make a pro-industry stance somehow "un-professional." Second, with no established professional network, the regulator hoping to move on must look closely at the job opportunities presented by the industry he or she regulates and that glance may dampen some of the individual's regulatory zeal.

Wilson is probably right that capture is an overstatement of the closeness of regulator-regulated relationships. Still, the CAB served airline interests for most of its life, the ICC was much more concerned about keeping long haul trucking profitable than shipping costs down, and the Securities and Exchange Commission has done well by New York Stock Exchange member firms. Each was dealing with a single industry it was supposed to promote as well as regulate. Each operated from no specific professional base, and each dealt in the realm of economics. Close cooperation was the result.

Not all regulation is economic, nor are all regulators lawyers gaining important, and marketable, experience. Some agencies are created to preserve or protect public health and safety, turned loose on most of the economy, and staffed by men and women who have found a professional calling. Such agencies often have a great deal of trouble getting along with the people and/or industries they regulate.

Responsibility for (jurisdiction over) the whole of American industry means less contact with any one set of industrial executives or representatives. This probably means a bit less familiarity with and sympathy for industry viewpoints. Far more important, however, are the professional basis and non-economic character of much of this multi-industry regulation.

Those who must issue regulations that protect public health and safety are in an ambiguous, probably ironic situation. The stakes involved go far beyond a piddling redistribution of income. When we talk about health and safety we are talking about priceless commodities. This time somebody just might die. But even though the benefits are priceless—literally no price tag can be put on them—the costs are so clearly and easily identified, categorized, and priced. Regulators are trapped. A pro-industry stance might leave some people sick, injured, perhaps even dead, but an anti-industry stance, which might prevent these things, is certain to be costly and almost as certain to bring down the organized wrath of whatever industry is being "pushed around."

Now pile on the sometimes overlooked impact of professionalism. If the regulators are drawn from a distinct profession created to do this sort of regulation, or even from one that has co-opted this regulatory activity as its own, there is a set of norms and standards by which regulation is to be conducted and by which regulators will be judged by their professional peers. Pride and job prospects will then combine to put tremendous pressure on regulators to act in a professional manner.

This is not to say that no true professional would ever take a pro-industry position nor that any reasonable human being would choose health and safety over profits no matter what the costs. But, if the essence of the profession is regulation, that is, designing rules and procedures for doing certain things, then the norms and standards of that profession are by definition pro-regulation. In the contemporary climate, that is bound to be seen as anti-business. In addition, it is true that lots of people might choose profits over safety or, more properly, choose a mixture of profits and safety with considerable emphasis on the former and very little on the latter. But they are not the kinds of people likely to be attracted to a career (profession) in health or safety regulation.

Steven Kelman's research reveals the Occupational Safety and Health Administration to be a classic example of all of the ingredients that lead to hostility between regulators and regulated.[14] OSHA's mandate reaches all of American business and industry, and safety and health are all-inclusive terms, at least if you want them to be. But at the heart of the matter is a heavy dose of professionalism, both in the sense of conformance to the norms, procedures, and viewpoints that define appropriate professional conduct and in the less flattering sense of protecting professional turf. Kelman finds plenty of both on one of the key questions OSHA confronts, namely, the choice between personal safety equipment and factory redesign. Consider the following: "The view that hazards should be corrected by means other than personal protective equipment is a dictum of these [safety engineering or industrial hygiene] professions. Nearly every textbook on safety engineering or industrial hygiene is replete with warnings against reliance on personal protective equipment. . . . An engineering-controls approach [also] encourages participation by safety and health professionals during the planning stage and upgrades their role within the organization."[15] Indeed, Kelman is so convinced of the importance of this professional dimension that he concludes that the "ideology of the occupational safety and health professions"[16] is the most important force behind OSHA's consistently pro-protection outlook, the very outlook that causes so much conflict between the agency and the business and industrial community.

One of the many spots on the continuum from the Civil Aeronautics Board of the late 1960's to the OSHA of the late 1970's is occupied by the Nuclear Regulatory Commission. Regulating, and in a very real sense promoting, a single industry, the NRC is susceptible to coziness in its relationship with the nuclear power industry. Part of NRC regulation is economic—the license to operate—but the bulk is safety-related (how a plant is to be operated) and the NRC has nothing to say about the price of the resulting electricity. There is a profession—nuclear engineering —and while it may not exhibit the single-minded dedication of the industrial hygiene community, it is surely safety conscious. In short, the NRC is a mixed bag and the mixture is reflected in its relations with the industry. Long license delays and occasional shutdowns have frustrated power companies and cost a good deal of money, but the famous "spent fuel cycle rule" (lack of a waste disposal plan was held insufficient grounds for license denial) and the near gutting of post-Three Mile Island safety restrictions were seen by many as classic cases of regulators giving in to those they regulate.

Agencies generally get along with their clientele groups. It pays dividends and the two tend to be a lot alike anyway. But for some agencies, cooperation with clientele may not feel so good. For some it is because their clients are very different from themselves and have no political power or legitimacy to offer the agency as part of a mutually satisfying trade. For others, it is because of the nature of the task—regulation—and of the circumstances in which the task must be performed.

Bureaucrats and Professional Associations

According to Herbert Kaufman, "The professions strongly represented in its work force" constitute one of the two most consistent sets of supporters a bureau possesses.[17] Among the major elements in the political environment of the Forest Service, Kaufman listed associations of professional foresters and schools of forestry and environmental sciences, while among the key groups associated with the Agriculture Department's Animal and Plant Health Inspection Service (APHIS) were included veterinarians and schools of veterinary medicine, and among those dealing with the Internal Revenue Service he found "associations and schools for accountants, lawyers, and other tax preparers."[18] In fact, as noted earlier, Frederick Mosher has carried the argument even further, contending that the professionalization of government activity has reached the point at which, "in a good many cases, the goals and standards of public agencies, as seen by their officers and employees, are identical with the goals and standards of the professions as they are seen by their members."[19]

Once again, the bonds of self-interest and empathy hold fast.

Professional associations clearly cannot supply an agency with the kind of power its clientele groups can, but they can provide a valuable increment to an agency's power base. As supposedly neutral experts, they have a kind of credibility that clientele groups often lack. When trade associations representing beef, poultry, or pork growers try to influence APHIS policies, they are assumed simply to be out to make a profit. When veterinarians try, they are perceived as trying to protect the health of the animals and ultimately of the people who will consume the hamburgers, steaks, and chops. APHIS needs the support of both the hog growers and the veterinarians.

Professional associations also stand to benefit from close co-operation with "their" agencies. Some of the benefits are economic. Agencies provide consulting opportunities, advisory board appointments, research grants, and one of the best sources of job opportunities for the next generation of fellow professionals. I am convinced, however, that the most important benefits to professional associations are personal and professional benefits to association members. These men and women honestly care about what government does in this little corner of the world. On a personal level, this caring may be what drew these people to their profession in the first place, and on a professional level they believe fervently in their expert knowledge and the contribution it can make to the development of sound public policy. Some may even enjoy the feeling of being involved in the "real world" of policy formation. In any event, close working relationships between professional associations and government agencies allow association members to fulfill some fairly important goals and that means that veterinarians need APHIS as much as APHIS needs the vets.

Anyone serving on a university faculty knows that pretty dissimilar folks can choose the same profession. Still, shared professional commitments—in particular the most basic one of all, commitment to the use of specialized knowledge to find correct answers—breed some sort of empathy between agency staff and professional association members. In addition, there is bound to be a good bit of personal/professional interaction between the two, since agency types are likely to be members of the associations themselves. Finally, Frederick Mosher is probably right that, "over the long pull, the most profound impact upon the professional public services is that of the Universities—their professional schools, their departments in the physical and social sciences which produce professionals, and their faculties in general. Higher education produces the bulk of future professionals. By their images, and by their impressions on students, the schools have a great influence on who opts for what fields and what kinds of young people—of what quality, what interests, what values—go where. It is clear too that they influence the choices by students among employers—whether government or other, and which jurisdictions and agencies of government." [20] Professionals in and out of government think and feel a lot alike.

Bureaucrats and Individual Policy Experts

Finally, a good many agencies draw some support from individual citizens duly certified as policy experts. Many of these individuals come from the ranks of former government officials, the rest from universities and non-profit research organizations.

Former government officials often come with expert credentials and carefully nurtured contacts developed over long and often successful careers. Their support for an agency can be quite helpful. Likewise their opposition can hurt, as Stanford G. Ross found out when he sought to make dramatic changes in Social Security Administration policies. Ross, appointed Social Security Commissioner in 1978, was highly critical of former Commissioner Robert M. Ball. A number of Ross's initiatives were blunted, in part, according to Herbert Kaufman, because "Ball and Cohen [Wilbur J. Cohen, long time SSA official and former HEW Secretary] out of office still commanded attention in the relevant committees of Congress." [21] Mr. Ball still does. He was a key member of the special commission that designed the 1983 "bail out" of the Social Security System. [22]

Subject matter specialists from universities or the various policy think tanks may not have the contacts or even reputation of some former government officials, but they generally have a good bit of credibility, and credibility can be a useful political resource. These experts are the individual entrepreneurs of knowledge. They have no "axe to grind" on behalf of any interest group, no stake in defending past policies. At least that is the way they present themselves and the way they are often perceived.

Both sets of experts derive personal and professional benefits from working closely with agencies in their particular subject matter specialties. Former officials can continue to influence policies they have devoted so much to. Or they can defend them from reformers. Besides, lots of these men and women have a low-grade strain of "Potomac Fever." They just want to keep on being part of the action. Policy specialists who have not been part of government gain the personal and professional satisfaction of involvement in policies that matter so much to them and, maybe, the added benefit of insider status and a little prestige back home.

Finally, these people, too, feel good about each other. The former officials were once insiders and almost certainly worked closely with today's insiders. The relationship just continues in a slightly different form. University and research organization specialists are not really former colleagues, but they are hardly outsiders. As noted in the previous section, professionals in and out of government really do think and feel a lot alike. It's true even if those outside have never been inside.

Bureaucrats and Their Critics

Not all of those who care about an agency's decisions are to be found among its supporters. According to Herbert Kaufman, the U.S. Forest Service faces "some organizations against all man induced change in vast areas of the public domain [which] were apt to fight every measure for development of the resources in those properties and to denounce any public official and agency not similarly inclined."[23] Individual citizens can get in on the critic act, too, as John Banzhaff has done in his two-decade-long war against cigarettes. Whether it be the isolated voice of Rachel Carson or the Greek chorus of the Sierra Club, most agencies are going to hear from some dissatisfied people. Their response is mixed. The relationship that results is one of contentious accommodation.

Close cooperation is pretty much out of the question. Neither side could really afford it. Agencies would find the demands of these individuals and groups so much at odds with those of their clientele and professional supporters that it would be impossible to be responsive to the critics without angering their traditional supporters. If the Forest Service kept the Sierra Club and the Wilderness Society happy with its management of eastern Washington's Kaniksu National Forest, there is no doubt that Weyerhauser and Georgia Pacific would be seething. So would the Society of American Foresters. Its members manage timber resources; they don't save trees.

But the Sierra Club or Wilderness Society leadership couldn't handle a close and cooperative relationship with the Forest Service either. Critics cannot maintain credibility with their followers—group membership or just "fellow travelers"—if they become insiders. They cannot maintain credibility with themselves either. Most of these critics are critics by choice. They are interested in a subject and dissatisfied with the way in which the government is handling that subject. Many have also developed the personal style of the critic, never satisfied, always questioning. Becoming an insider would mean changing tunes and styles, and the critics would have to find a rationalization for doing so that the critics themselves could swallow. That may not be as easy as it sounds.

In effect, each side needs to keep its distance from the other. In fact, they need to keep the sparks flying. Agencies have to show their supporters that they are out there fighting for shared values. Critics need to show their supporters—and themselves—that they haven't sold out. The easiest way for each of them to do it is to slug it out.

Neither side minds fighting all that much since they don't particularly care for each other. Critics often see agency staff as tools of their clientele, defining the public interest narrowly and pursuing that definition blindly. They frequently say so. That grates on agency personnel, who see themselves as professionals producing policies based on careful and systematic analysis. They see a lot of that criticism as unfair. Besides, it hurts. So the two sides don't like each other all that much and a good fight seems to feel just right.

Agencies win more of these fights than they lose, but they don't want to win them all. As Herbert Kaufman put it, "The bureaus did not ignore [hostile groups], however. In the first place, the arguments of the hostile groups often had merit, so the sensible course was to hear them out and to respond to their valid contentions as far as possible. Second, the consistently critical groups bombarded the bureau's normal allies with their materials, so the bureaus were obliged to analyze and evaluate their argument to make sure bureau supporters heard both sides of every issue. And third, refusal to yield an inch to these critics was seen as lending credibility to their charges that the agencies were bureaucratically rigid [or to charges of being a mere clientele servant]. So the bureaus not only heard them out, but tried to rebut their contentions and accommodate to them whenever possible. *Unlike the relationships with natural allies, these relationships were thrust on the bureaus rather than eagerly seized or initiated and cultivated by them.*" [24]

Needless to say, nobody likes to lose all the time. Even the most determined of individual critics needs an occasional victory to sustain his or her thirst for the battle, and the men and women who represent groups organized to criticize government policy need a few wins to demonstrate to the members whose time, effort, and dollars keep the organization going that theirs is not an exercise in futility. Whether representing groups of like-minded people or just strongly held personal feelings, bureaucracy's critics are not talking merely to hear their own voices. They want to influence policy and they must have an occasional success to keep them going.

So neither side is all that fond of the other, and each needs a good fight to prove to itself, and to others, that it is doing what it is supposed to do. Critics need to win once in a while, but strange as it sounds, agencies need to lose once in a while. The result is a mutually satisfying relationship best described by the term contentious accommodation.

Bureaucrats and the General Public

Finally, there is the general public. Though no one seems able to define it successfully, we all seem to agree that "the public interest" means something different from the demands of the "special interests" and that it is the former that should be the foundation stone for all public policy. At least we all agree on that until it is time to make specific decisions that will affect real people. In any event, there is supposed to be something called the general public and there definitely are organizations called public interest groups that claim to represent its true concerns and interests, so bureaucrats have to figure out how to respond.

In a sense, bureaucrats and the general public ignore each other. It's not terribly difficult to understand why.

For its part, the general public has almost no incentive to do otherwise.[25] The Bureau of Land Management does spend "our" money and does decide who can use 284 million acres of "our" land for what purposes. But it doesn't require much money from any one of us and most of us have never seen "our" land. For that matter, most of us have no idea that we own all of that land and no real concern about what it is used for. Nor are we all that much interested in the Bureau of Reclamation's fifty-three hydroelectric plants, its thousands of miles of irrigation ditches, or even its ("our") multi-billion-dollar investment in Western agriculture. Only a tiny handful of agencies have a direct and observable impact on the lives of most Americans and even these few seem remote from the everyday world and hardly susceptible to our influence. There seems no reason whatever to organize and try to have some impact on what most agencies are doing.

That is in stark contrast to the situation of agency clientele and professional supporters, of course, since as we saw in the previous section, these groups have a great deal to gain if they can mold the policies of "their" agencies to their own advantage. There is a good deal of money to be made on "our" 284 million acres, and a five-mile canal can turn desert into profitable farm-land, so some people have a great deal at stake when the BLM decides whether or not to open certain tracts of land for mineral exploration or how much timber should come from a particular forest, and others have a similar interest when the Bureau of Reclamation decides how many canals should be dug this year and where they will be, settles on a price for the water that will flow through the canals, and enforces the rules for buying into this publicly subsidized water supply system.

On the other side, bureaucracy has no more incentive to listen to the general public than the general public has to holler at the bureaucrats. In fact, incentive is probably irrelevant, since most agencies could listen all day and would still never hear a single word from the general public. As Herbert Kaufman put it, "The administrators heard from self-selected, interested parties, not from the general public, though all the special groups in the congressional, executive, nongovernmental and other sets of in-terests claimed at various times to speak for 'it.' And because 'it' encompassed such diverse and mutually incompatible interests, nobody could reasonably argue that 'it' wanted something, let alone what that something was." [26]

In the end, bureaucrats do ignore the general public, but only rarely in the sense that they hear from that public and decide they prefer the views of clientele and professional supporters. They simply don't hear because no one is talking.

The general public itself may speak to bureaucrats in a deaf-ening silence, but Public Citizen, Common Cause, the League of Women Voters, and the American Civil Liberties Union can make a good bit of noise when they want to. Though it may sound strange at first, not all that much of that noise is directed at bureaucrats.

The term public interest group has become a fairly elastic one. It had to to cover all the groups that have claimed it. I believe it ought to be used in a far more restrictive way; that is, I would prefer to stick all of the groups that zero in on a specific set of issues and agencies in the category of critical groups discussed in the previous section and reserve the title public interest group for the more general umbrella organizations such as Common Cause or the League of Women Voters. Critical Mass, the Nader-sponsored group that devotes its time and energy to the issue of nuclear power, is a good example of why. Critical Mass may indeed represent the public interest. It surely represents the view of that interest shared by its staff and members. Nonetheless, by virtue of the fact that it selects a fairly narrow range of issues, hires professional staff versed in those issues, and pursues its objectives by a relentless drumbeat of criticism of the Nuclear Regulatory Commission, it becomes something very different from Common Cause and the like.

If you accept this narrower definition of the term, then public interest groups turn out to be a pretty unimportant part of the bureaucrat's political environment. Most of them do not direct their attention to specific agencies and specific policies. According to Norman Ornstein and Shirley Elder, Common Cause "has focused its efforts on governmental and institutional reform."[27] The League of Women Voters, on the other hand, "directs its attention to public political education . . . though it also lobbies on issues such as governmental reform and the Equal Rights Amendment."[28] Public Citizen Litigation Group is something of an exception since it may sue any agency at any time over any decision. But most of these suits are sparked by the critical groups that are part of the Nader orbit, so agencies need not worry about PCLG coming out of nowhere. They'll hear the thunder first.

The general public doesn't know or care much about bureaucracy and those I have left in the category of public interest groups are directing their efforts elsewhere. None of this means the general public is being sold out, that its interests are known and ignored. It is hard to say if most bureaucrats believe there is no such thing as the general public interest or believe, as Herbert Kaufman does, that they are actually being responsive to it whatever it is.[29] In practical terms it probably doesn't much matter. Either way, the general public and its self-appointed spokesmen have very little direct influence over bureaucratic decision making.

Methods of Public Influence

Only rarely does the public, in any of its possible forms, possess legal authority over the activities of executive branch agencies. The public does not write agency budgets, oversee program implementation, or manipulate the formal administrative structure. But the absence of legal authority hardly implies an absence of influence. The public can exercise some indirect influence over bureaucracy through the Congress and the President, and some direct opportunities are also available, informally by lobbying the various agencies and formally through service on advisory committees, appearances at public hearings, or the filing of statements or position papers during the notice and comment period that is part of the bureaucratic rule-making process. Finally, though it is quite rare, specific segments of the public may be granted a formal, legally sanctioned, role in the design and implementation of programs that directly affect them. Farmer-elected Stabilization and Conservation Committees play a crucial role in Department of Agriculture-run price support and set aside programs, and locally elected committees of stockmen are directly involved in the BLM's grazing programs.

Indirect Public Influence

The public can influence bureaucratic policy making through the power it can muster in Congress and with the President. But the point of the previous two chapters has been that these two institutions exercise what power they can muster over bureaucracy in such a way that the result is a consistent pattern of clientele influence over agency decision making.

By delegating its powers of oversight and personnel selection, along with its control over administrative structure and most of its legislative authority to authorizing committees and subcommittees closely allied with agency clientele groups, Congress virtually guaranteed indirect clientele influence over bureaucracy. The choice was deliberate—look how the Congress prevented the non-clientele-dominated Government Operations Committees from mounting an effective challenge in the areas of administrative structure and oversight. The benefits that accrue to subcommittee members have already been discussed, so all that needs to be noted here is the fact that Congress uses its direct legal authority over bureaucracy to ensure that clientele groups have plenty of indirect influence over the agencies that serve or regulate them.

The President's relationship with the bureaucracy also results in indirect clientele influence over agency decision making. Here it is less a matter of power than of weakness, less a contribution of conscious effort than of inadvertence. The Chief Executive does not have the tools to counter the forces pushing toward clientele influence. Agencies define the public interest in terms of the interests of their support groups and Congress simultaneously gives the agencies the power to resist their "Chief" and withholds from him the means to overcome that resistance. There is ample reason to wonder if a President would make a serious effort to counter clientele influence over bureaucratic agencies even if he had the ability to do so. Presidents do not ignore the political or the ethical claims of organized interests and frequently conclude that most agencies, clientele groups, and the issues that arouse their passionate concern are just not worth a Chief Executive's time and energy. Even where opportunities exist to counter clientele-oriented patterns of appointment to top executive branch posts, Presidents seldom use them.[30]

The Congress does it deliberately and systematically, the President more or less inadvertently, but the result is the same. Their authority over executive branch agencies produces a substantial amount of indirect clientele influence over program implementation.

Direct Public Influence: The Informal Side

Bureaucrats, like members of Congress, engage in a good deal of informal give and take with the public. Most of that give and take, of course, takes place between agency staff and the leaders of that agency's clientele groups or other traditional supporters. As Herbert Kaufman noted, the informal communications channels between executive branch agencies and their support groups are always open.[31] In addition, these groups do engage in lobbying activities, though I suspect that both sides would be quite uncomfortable with the term lobbying and its connotation of putting "pressure" on the agency. When it comes from friends of long standing, it just doesn't feel like pressure. Often as not, agency officials will solicit clientele and other professional reaction to policy and program alternatives facing the agency and that reaction will be an important factor in the final decision. Whatever they choose to call it, direct face to face contacts, in which group representatives present their group's viewpoint and agency officials pay close attention to what they hear, are part of the daily world of most executive branch units, and they constitute an important source of clientele influence over bureaucracy.[32]

Also, most agency careerists come to identify with the interests of their support groups, especially with those of their traditional clientele. As I argued earlier, this intense identification is the result of the play of social, cultural, professional, political, and even philosophical forces. It can occur almost imperceptibly, but when it does it exerts a powerful pull on an agency's personnel. Once these men and women begin to think of the agency and its clientele as one—one set of people, one set of interests—then clientele concerns become the focal point of agency decision making. Agency staff adopt clientele interests as their own and proceed to weigh alternatives, make recommendations, and implement programs on the basis of the impact they might have on those interests. It is not just difficult for us to "know where the group leaves off and the agency begins"[33]; it is difficult for the agency itself.

Direct Public Influence: The Formal Side

A lot of the influence the public is able to exercise over bureaucracy is exercised indirectly and a good bit more informally as agency staff listen to the many voices of that public. Still, we should not overlook the formal avenues for public participation in, and influence over, agency decision making. Most agencies are required, either by the Administrative Procedure Act or the agency's own enabling legislation, to inform the public of rules it wishes to promulgate or cases it intends to decide, and then to offer the opportunity for public comment and criticism. In some cases, the agency will even be required to hold a full-scale public hearing. I will consider the question of the impact of these requirements in the next chapter, but there can be no doubt that they do offer some sort of avenue for the public to try to influence agency activity. In addition, a substantial number of agencies have created formal advisory committees. Over 1,500 such committees currently offer all sorts of advice to agencies from the Forest Service to the Center for Disease Control and in the process open up one more formal opportunity for public influence over bureaucracy.

These formal mechanisms are not quite as thoroughly clientele-dominated as are the informal and the indirect channels of public influence. Nearly every advisory committee will have a few members appointed to be "representative of the general public," and the Federal Advisory Committee Act of 1972 mandates that "Committee meetings shall be open to the public and fairly balanced in terms of points of view represented and the functions to be performed."[34] Advisory committees may even contain a critic or two—nutritionist Michael Jacobson offers his advice to the FDA—but even if not, the formal devices of written comment during the notice and comment period and/or testimony at public hearings are definitely open to the critical groups and individuals and they use them.

The formal channels of influence may be less dominated by traditional agency support groups, but this does not mean that these groups cannot or do not use them very effectively. For every real live critic on an agency advisory committee there will be a handful of clientele and professional supporters, and the so-called public members will often drown in a sea of insider jargon and incomprehensible reports. The notice and comment period will elicit tons of paper from agency supporters just as public hearings will find lots of tried and true agency friends on the docket and in the audience. It is also important to remember that while a bureaucrat is legally obligated to read the comments and listen to the testimony, there is and can be no obligation to give any of it the slightest credence. The comments of long-time friends, based on shared values and commitments and couched in familiar terms, are almost certain to get a better hearing.

Given the influence they can exercise outside these formal channels, one might reasonably wonder why agency support groups would feel the need to use them at all. In fact, both David Truman[35] and Harold Seidman[36] have argued that the danger of becoming identified with policies they oppose could create a serious problem for many clientele group and professional association leaders when they agree to advisory committee service. Truman and Seidman may be correct, but most of the 1,500 formal advisory bodies currently in operation are the province of the clientele groups, professional associations, and individual experts normally associated with the agency or department on the receiving end of the committee's advice, and I believe the reason is simple. These advisory committees are a key ingredient in the quest for legitimacy, by both sides.

Clientele groups are, after all, organized interest groups, nobody's favorite political actors. When a clientele group representative states his or her group's position to an agency official in the privacy of that official's office, it may be considered "lobbying" and a favorable response thought of as giving in to pressure. Neither side believes that policy should be influenced by "interest group pressures." Both are convinced it should be made after a search for the technically or professionally appropriate course of action. Due regard should be given to the interests of the people directly affected by the policy (who just happen to be the agency's clientele), but "interest group pressure" has no legitimate place. Moving some of the agency-clientele relationship out into the open and formalizing it through advisory committee service, written memoranda during the notice and comment period, and appearances at public hearings is a step on the path from "interest group pressure" to "public input" and that is an important path for both sides to tread.

Through hearings, written comments, and occasionally even service on one of the many agency advisory committees, the public has the opportunity to influence bureaucratic policy making. These formal mechanisms provide a way for agency critics and possibly the general public to have some say over what specific agencies do, but even though these channels may not be dominated by traditional bureaucratic support groups, there is still plenty of room for those groups to make themselves heard. They use it.

Formal Program Authority

Though the practice is rare and largely confined to the area of agriculture policy, we do occasionally find the ultimate in public influence over bureaucracy, a direct, legally sanctioned role in program design and implementation. The price support system, the operation of the Farm Credit Administration (before 1986), and the Bureau of Land Management-run grazing program, all grant legal authority to the clientele groups affected by program decisions.

Each of the approximately 2,800 agricultural counties in the United States has a Stabilization and Conservation Committee. The members of the Committee are elected by the farmers of that particular county and possess the legal authority to "make new allotments, work out adjustments and review complaints regarding allotments, determine whether quotas have been complied with, inspect and approve storage facilities, and perform as the court of original jurisdiction on violations of price support rules and on eligibility for parity payments." [37] From the point of view of any one farmer, these are crucial decisions, and they certainly appear to be the essence of policy implementation and administration in the price support system. As Theodore Lowi concludes, "Congress determines the general level of supports, and the Secretary of Agriculture proclaims the national acreage quotas for adjusting the supply to the guaranteed price. But the locally elected committees stand between the farmer and Washington." [38]

The Farm Credit Administration is an independent agency of the federal government that oversees the activities of a loose collection of lending institutions that together comprise the cooperative Farm Credit System.[39] From the early 1950's until December 1985, all Farm Credit Administration policies were set by a thirteen-member part-time board, composed of one individual chosen by the Secretary of Agriculture and twelve chosen by the more conventional route of presidential nomination and Senate confirmation. The list of nominees from which the President was to select "his" twelve board members was submitted to him by "the national farm loan associations, the production credit associations, and the cooperatives who are stockholders of or subscribers to the guaranty fund of the bank for cooperatives." [40] This board then appointed the FCA's chief executive officer. The 1953 law that set all of this in motion further required that the FCA governor comply with all board orders and directives.[41] For thirty years the whole system belonged to the farm lenders who were part of it.

But the farm credit crisis of the mid-1980's gave Ronald Reagan the leverage he needed, and in exchange for the President's agreement to allow the infusion of some badly needed capital into the Farm Credit System, Congress agreed to abolish the part-time board and replace it with a three-member full-time board. Both the board members and the governor will be selected by the customary process of presidential nomination and Senate confirmation.[42]

Finally, the Bureau of Land Management uses locally elected committees of ranchers much like the County Stabilization and Conservation Committees that help to run the price support/ acreage allotment system for the DOA. These Grazing District Committees have a substantial amount of authority and even do a good bit of the day to day administration of the grazing program, including the determination of the number of head a particular rancher will be permitted to graze on BLM-managed land.[43]

Direct delegation of program authority to clientele groups is not common. With the Farm Credit Administration's reorganization the list is growing shorter and there haven't been many additions lately. The House of Representatives tried in 1982, when it passed the plan for a new National Dairy Board. The Board, to be comprised exclusively of milk producers—the plan originated with the National Milk Producers Federation, after all—would have been empowered to set a new price support level for surplus milk and oversee the management of that surplus. The statute defined surplus as anything over that which would be used domestically, plus 5 billion pounds.[44] The Reagan Administration opposed the plan and the Senate turned it down, so maybe the idea of direct delegation of authority to clientele group representatives is losing favor even in its traditional home in agriculture.

Summary and Conclusion

The public really does exercise a great deal of influence over the federal bureaucracy, or at least some people do. That influence is agency and/or subject matter specific — that is, nobody influences every agency, but every agency is influenced by somebody — and some people have a whole lot more of it than do others, but influence there is.

Most agencies listen to a comfortable circle of friends and supporters. With some understandable exceptions for agencies providing services to certain kinds of people and those operating in a particular regulatory context, the most consistent set of supporters for any agency is to be found among its clients. People whose economic — or other — interests are directly affected by an agency's decisions will almost certainly organize (if they can) and try to work closely with their agency in order to be able to leave some mark on those decisions. Agencies, too, derive substantial benefits from working closely with these groups and this mutual self-interest is supplemented by more personal ties to establish a relationship satisfying to both sides. Groups of people with a professional interest in an agency's subject matter responsibilities will also seek to join that agency in its policy-making activities. The stakes are different, but no less important, and the two — agency and professional association — generally get along extremely well. Finally, some individual policy experts will try to become part of this durable policy-making partnership. There will be internal squabbles, and, for a time at least, relationships may be strained, but year in and year out an agency can count on these same people and those people can count on the agency. Their influence is felt.

Most agencies also listen to their critics. It isn't anywhere near as much fun and no agency will ever be as responsive to those critics as it is to its support groups, but listen it must. A good fight beforehand allows both agency and critics to maintain credibility in their respective camps, and an occasional victory for the Sierra Club or Critical Mass is beneficial not just to that particular group but to the agency that "lost." It really is a mutually satisfying relationship.

Finally, most agencies do not listen to the general public. For most agencies no such public exists, or, at least, there is no way to know what it wants. The public at large may well have a tremendous stake in the policies of a particular agency, but with the stake of each individual in that public so very low and with the level of knowledge and interest for each individual even lower, it isn't hard to see why it is virtually impossible to mobilize that public to get it to speak to the bureaucracy. Whether it would be heard anyway is an interesting question, but since it almost never speaks, it is a pretty safe bet it isn't heard now.

It should come as no surprise at all that an agency's clientele groups will use their influence with that agency to advance their own interests. They will call it The Public Interest, of course, but what they are defending is the group's interest.

Professional associations and individual policy experts are no less zealous protectors of their own interests and no less likely to call it The Public Interest than are an agency's clientele groups. Generally the interests they are protecting are more psychological than economic—that is, they are defending *right* (expert-derived) answers and occasionally even the very principle of expert knowledge as the proper guide for policy making—but they are no less dedicated, or narrow minded, than are those groups and individuals who are defending their economic interests.

In a good many instances, there may be considerable overlap between the professional associations with which a particular agency's staff identifies and that agency's clientele groups. Weyerhauser and Georgia Pacific—two of the giants of the timber industry—employ a good many professional foresters. Graduates of accredited forestry programs, the same ones that Forest Service personnel attended, these professional foresters belong to the Society of American Foresters, as do the professional staffs of the major timber industry trade associations. Weyerhauser and Georgia Pacific also employ consultants, generally professors from the nation's leading schools of forestry, professors who play prominent roles in the Society of American Foresters as well as in the training of the next generation of professional foresters. This is not to say that the Society of American Foresters acts as a mouthpiece for the timber industry. But there is a good deal of overlap between professional association and clientele, an overlap not just of members but of interests. They tend to see The Public Interest through very similar eyes and that tends to reinforce the belief of all of these policy-making partners that their shared interests really are the only ones that need to be brought to bear on the decisions they are called upon to make.

Critics, too, represent their own interests and are even more determined to call it The Public Interest. Not only that, they say it louder. Whether these groups are any closer to The Public Interest or not is a matter of opinion, but their claim to the mantle rests on ground very similar to that of the clientele–professional association alliance. They have simply taken it. I tend to sympathize with the Sierra Club far oftener than I do with Weyerhauser, but even though I have deputized that environmental watchdog to speak for me, I can't deputize it to speak for The Public. I'm not sure who can.

Once again, as I said at the end of the previous chapter, clientele group and professional association interests are legitimate interests that deserve a prominent place in an agency's decision calculus. But they don't deserve to be there alone. The evidence suggests that, all too often, they are.

Bureaucracy and the Law

T he legal system offers one more avenue for influence over bureaucratic policy making. More properly, it offers two avenues. First of all, no matter what an agency is about to decide, there are rules about how that decision is to be made. These rules—known collectively as administrative law—can be found in the Administrative Procedure Act, in authorizing statutes, in court opinions, and even in an agency's own regulations. The rules vary from agency to agency and from one type of decision to another, but rules there are and agencies feel a strong obligation to play by them. The result is some definite impact on what bureaucracy does and how it does it. Second, every agency knows that it might be called upon to defend any decision it makes in a court of law. Citizens angry over a decision to license a nuclear power plant, or one to allow clear cutting in a particular national forest, or one specifying the minimum peanut content in peanut butter may sue the offending agency. If they do, the agency must come before a judge and explain what was decided, why it was decided, and how it was decided. If the judge isn't happy with the decision or the agency's explanation of the how or why of it, he or she may tell that agency to try again. This, too, means some external influence over bureaucratic decision making.

Bureaucrats and the Courts

Back in the late 1960's, Walt Disney Enterprises wanted to build a major resort in the Mineral King Valley of California's Sierra Nevada mountain range. Because most of the valley is either national forest or national park land, the Disney folks needed permission from the U.S. Forest Service and the Department of Interior. They got it, but the Sierra Club was upset enough about the whole affair to sue.[1] Right around the same time, the Department of Transportation highway planners and Secretary of Transportation John Volpe agreed with the City Council of Memphis Tennessee that Interstate 40 ought to go through Overton Park, not around it. Secretary Volpe soon found himself in court answering a suit brought by a group called Citizens to Preserve Overton Park.[2]

The list goes on. Thousands of times every year bureaucrats are called into court to explain what they have done and why what they have done was wise, prudent, and done within the confines of the law. Bureaucrats win some of these challenges. The American Textile Manufacturers Institute was extremely unhappy with the Occupational Safety and Health Administration's rule limiting the concentrations of cotton dust in the air of textile mills. The Institute's subsequent suit got all the way to the Supreme Court, but the rule was upheld.[3] Bureaucrats also lose some of these challenges. Only a year before OSHA won on the challenge to its cotton dust rule, it had lost on a challenge to a rule limiting the concentration of benzene gas in the air of oil refineries and other factories.[4]

So bureaucrats do get hauled into court to defend their decisions and they aren't always able to do so successfully. Despite the fact that an agency loss is by definition an instance of external control over bureaucracy, the courts will never become an effective and systematic check on bureaucratic decision making. Judges cannot overturn a decision they have never looked at, and most bureaucratic decisions are never subjected to judicial review.

First of all, Congress keeps the courts from reviewing an awful lot of agency decisions. Section 701 of the Administrative Procedure Act precludes review of decisions in two sets of circumstances, namely, when an agency's authorizing statute prohibits such review — 701(a)(1) — and when "agency action is committed to agency discretion by law" — 701(a)(2). There is a good bit of confusion as to when agency action is committed to agency discretion by law, but there is no doubt that Congress has put some agency actions outside the scope of judicial review. It has done so directly and quite explicitly as it did in a 1970 statute exempting a number of Veterans Administration decisions from legal challenge, and it has done so indirectly as it did by refusing to repeal an 1862 statute limiting attorney's fees in veterans benefits challenges to ten dollars.[5]

Second, courts keep themselves from reviewing certain bureaucratic decisions. If, during the course of litigation, the harm alleged by the plaintiff ceases, the case becomes moot and the courts will almost certainly refuse to decide it. For example, the University of Washington Law School's affirmative action admissions program was challenged by a white male denied entry to the school. The student, Marco DeFunis, was admitted under a temporary injunction and by the time the case reached the Supreme Court, DeFunis was near the end of his final year and certain to be graduated. The Court refused to rule on the admissions system, eventually making Alan Bakke a star.[6] Standing — the right to bring suit against this particular action — is another traditional court gatekeeping rule that puts some decisions outside the scope of judicial review. It was the Sierra Club's standing, or lack of it, that was the key factor in the loss of its initial challenge to the Mineral King Valley resort.[7] Courts also won't review an agency action unless the individual complaining has exhausted every avenue of appeal within the agency and its parent department. Finally, cases must be ripe, that is, ready for judicial determination. As Justice Harlan put it, the doctrine of ripeness is essential "to prevent the courts, through avoidance of premature adjudication, from entangling themselves in abstract disagreements over administrative policies, and also to protect the agencies from judicial interference until an administrative decision has been formalized and its effects felt in a concrete way by the challenging party." [8]

None of these formal barriers would be impenetrable to a determined judge. The long and highly detailed preclusion of review clause in the 1970 Veterans Administration Act was a congressional response to the fact that judges had been allowing review of a sizable number of veterans benefits cases despite earlier congressional efforts to prevent it. [9] No matter how specific a preclusion clause may exist, the Supreme Court has held administrative actions reviewable if there is an allegation that the agency acted beyond or clearly departed from its statutory mandate. [10] Judges can avoid even their own self-imposed obstacles, since ripeness may well be in the eye of the beholder, and standing can be stretched pretty far, as it was when five law students were allowed to challenge freight rate increases approved by the Interstate Commerce Commission because "their members used the forests, streams, mountains, and other resources in the Washington metropolitan area for camping, hiking, fishing, and sightseeing, and that this use was disturbed by the adverse environmental impact caused by the nonuse of recyclable goods brought about by a rate increase on those commodities." [11]

Still, even if Ralph Nader should one day wake up to find himself Chief Judge of the D.C. Circuit, one formidable barrier to systematic judicial influence over administrative policy making would remain. Courts decide cases. Cases are the result of legal challenges, and as Florence Heffron observed, "Of the hundreds of thousands of administrative decisions made in a year, only a minuscule proportion will ever be reviewed." [12] It is true that the cases that are reviewed and decided will have some impact on decisions that are never contested. When the Supreme Court overturned OSHA's benzene rule, it told the agency that before any level was set it had to "make a threshold finding that a place of employment is unsafe—in the sense that significant risks are present and can be eliminated or lessened by a change in practice." [13] Ambiguous though it may be, OSHA knows this is to be taken as a general rule to guide future decisions and it has tried to comply. Still, Florence Heffron is clearly right when she says that we have no way "to determine how many of the vast majority of actions that are not challenged are legal, constitutional and proper." [14] The ones the courts decide affect the ones they never see, but it is impossible to say how many or how much.

It is clear that court rulings do have an effect on the content of specific bureaucratic decisions, sometimes even on entire areas of public policy. The Supreme Court prodded the old Federal Power Commission to a much more active role in the regulation of natural gas prices and used a judicial sledgehammer on the Federal Trade Commission.[15] Similarly, some lower federal courts were active enough in the substance of environmental policy that Mr. Justice Rehnquist felt compelled to point out the error of their ways in the *Vermont Yankee* opinion.[16] Nonetheless, Congress puts some bureaucratic decisions off limits to judges and the judges' own rules put some more decisions out of their reach. More important than both of these, of course, is the simple fact that most agency decisions are not met with a legal challenge. In the end, courts have some impact on administrative policy making, but that impact is a far cry from systematic and effective control over bureaucracy.

Bureaucracy and Administrative Law

For nearly anything an agency wants to do, there are rules about how to do it. With exceptions for internal management and personnel questions and a near blanket exemption for the protectors of national security, agencies are subject to the Administrative Procedure Act. Beyond that, many agencies find instructions about how to do what they do in their authorizing statutes.

The Environmental Protection Agency and the Federal Trade Commission have rather elaborate procedural guidelines built into the laws that created them. Some agencies go beyond the law to write their own rules for deciding the questions that come before them. Finally, courts impose procedural restrictions, as the Supreme Court did in 1970, when it ruled that New York could not terminate welfare benefits without providing the recipient with a formal pretermination hearing conducted in accordance with court-defined due process rules.[17]

Since three of these four sources of administrative law are agency specific, it is obvious that the rules for making decisions vary from one agency to another. The EPA is governed by a far tougher set of rules than the Immigration and Naturalization Service. But agency by agency variations are just the beginning of this patchwork quilt of procedures. Agencies make at least three fairly different kinds of decisions and the Administrative Procedure Act—and most of the rest of administrative law—spells out different rules for these different types of decisions.

First of all, agencies are sometimes called upon to act as highly specialized legislatures writing rules that will have the force of law within a particular area of policy. The EPA must say how much lead we can leave in the gasoline we burn and OSHA has to say how much cotton dust in the air of a textile mill is too much. Even within this general category of rule making, however, procedural requirements vary widely. By including the magic words "on the record, after opportunity for an agency hearing" in its authorizing statute, Congress can bring an agency's rule-making activities under the very formal and restrictive Sections 556 and 557 of the APA. At the opposite end of the spectrum are the rather loose requirements of Section 553. In between are the various hybrids created by Congress for specific agencies, or created by the agencies themselves as they supplemented the APA and their authorizing statutes. There are rules about how to make rules, but what the rules are depends on who the agency is and what sort of rule it wants to make.

Agencies are also called upon to decide specific cases involving specific industries, firms, or even individuals. Here they must enter the realm of contested facts and extenuating circumstances and eventually pass judgment and mete out punishment. The FCC had to decide if WSAW-TV in Wausau, Wisconsin, really was operated in the public interest between 1982 and 1985, and the NLRB had to determine if the New England Patriots drug-testing program was or was not an unfair labor practice. Once again, Congress can trigger a very formal process governed by APA Sections 554, 556 and 557 merely by speaking the magic words. If Congress remains silent, as it quite often does, agencies adopt their own rules within guidelines established by the courts. The most extensive and restrictive set of such guidelines can be found in the "Goldberg Rules," ten procedural requirements laid out by the Supreme Court in the 1970 case of *Goldberg v. Kelly*.[18] Subsequent cases, however, have made it clear that the Court will not demand that all agencies follow these rules when Congress has chosen not to impose the requirements of formal adjudication found in APA Sections 554, 556, and 557.[19]

Finally, some things that agencies do can't be classified as either rule making or adjudication. In some cases these things can only loosely be described as decision making at all. But they can be important. The head of our local Social Security Office has a weekly five-minute radio broadcast and writes a column on Social Security questions that appears each Wednesday in two area newspapers. Recipients and would-be recipients rely on both, just as taxpayers rely on the information they get when they call an Internal Revenue Service toll free number, or just as an Idaho farmer by the name of Merrill relied on the Federal Crop Insurance Corporation employee who told him his crop was indeed insurable.[20] Stakes in these kinds of actions can be pretty big. HEW Secretary Arthur Flemming's November 1959 announcement that some of the Washington-Oregon cranberry crop had been contaminated by pesticides cost cranberry growers an estimated $21.5 million, and the publicity—much of it in

FDA press releases—that accompanied the recall of Bon Vivant vichyssoise in 1971 eventually bankrupt the corporation.[21] Yet there are no procedural guidelines for writing a newspaper column, announcing the contamination of food, or answering questions over the phone. Mr. Merrill's crop was not insurable under FCIC regulations and the Supreme Court ruled he was not entitled to compensation.[22]

Leaving aside decisions made under no guidelines save the administrative conscience, and those made in accordance with a special congressionally designed process, we are left with four distinct types of decisions or, more properly, four types of decision-making processes, each governed by its own set of rules. Three of these—informal rule making, formal rule making, and formal adjudication—are governed by the Administrative Procedure Act, supplemented on occasion by agency policy or court decisions. The fourth, informal adjudication, is governed primarily by procedures adopted by the various agencies themselves, with, or without, a little help from the courts.

So we have different rules for different agencies, different rules for different types of decisions. But what do we have the rules for? What are they supposed to do? In general, of course, these rules are supposed to control bureaucracy, to move it toward a more democratically acceptable method of decision making. Specifically, we have long harbored the fear that bureaucracy is prone to make decisions in a manner that is biased, secretive, exclusive, and closed. The rules are designed to eliminate the bias and make the process open, inclusive, participatory, and ultimately accountable.

Reducing Bias

All value judgments produce biases and not all biases are bad. We expect judges to be biased in favor of individual liberties, the EPA in favor of protecting the environment, OSHA in favor of safe and healthy work places, and so on. What we don't want is the bias that causes a decision maker to block out all opposing points of view and ignore all counterevidence, in short, the bias that becomes blind prejudice. The law and the courts attempt to combat this sort of bias by imposing the requirements of an impartial decision maker and by restricting what the law calls "ex-parte" contacts.

EX-PARTE CONTACTS

Ex-parte contacts are communications between agency decision makers and an individual party interested in the outcome of a decision that agency is called upon to make. The important, and disturbing, thing about them is the fact that they take place off the record and that, as a result, other interested parties are not given the opportunity to see, evaluate, and rebut the content of such communications. According to the editors of the *Yale Law Journal*, "Permitting unrestricted ex-parte contacts involves three major costs: potential inaccuracy in agency fact finding; possible unfairness in giving certain interested parties special access to decision makers; and the risk of improper political influence."[23] That sounds an awful lot like a recipe for bias.

Formal adjudications must be conducted under the rules laid out in Section 554(d) of the Administrative Procedure Act, rules that forbid ex-parte contacts except where authorized by law for specific purposes. But the provisions of 554 apply only when authorizing statutes specifically invoke them. Consequently, there is a great deal of informal adjudication and there the rules vary widely. The Goldberg Rules do not really speak directly to the question of ex-parte contacts, and, in any event, the Supreme Court has said that not all adjudications require hearings and not all hearings must meet the Goldberg test.[24] Two of the Goldberg Rules—cross-examination of adverse witnesses and disclosure to the claimant of opposing evidence—are aimed in part at the problem presumed to accompany ex-parte contacts, that is, reliance on evidence from one source that is never brought out and subjected to criticism or refutation. A look at Paul Verkuil's study of informal adjudication procedures reveals that only nine of the forty-two programs required cross-examination and ten the disclosure of opposing evidence.[25] Allowing for some overlap, close to one-third of the programs provided one or the other of these protections, but ten or fewer provided both. One can lose a license to inspect grain storage facilities, a permit to fish for shrimp, or certification for a stockyard under the animal quarantine laws and never get a chance to contest the evidence that was used to reach those decisions.[26]

When we enter the realm of rule making, however, we find a very different story. Once again, the rules for formal rule making (Sections 556 and 557) place significant restrictions on ex-parte contacts. The decision is to be based on the record compiled—transcripts of all testimony, documents filed, et cetera—and all parties have an opportunity to enter things into that record. Should the agency find that its decision actually rests on something outside that record, it is required to provide any interested party "an opportunity to show the contrary" (556 e). There are a couple of loopholes there. The agency must admit that it has taken "official notice" of this particular material fact and some interested party must request the opportunity to counter it, but interested parties who have followed it this far are ready to request and most agency types will feel considerable pressure to play it straight by taking official notice of relevant facts not in the record. Finally, Section 557(d)(A) makes as strong a statement prohibiting ex-parte contacts as can be made.

Ex-parte contacts are rare in formal rule making, but, for better or worse, so is formal rule making itself. Just as Section 554 procedures for formal adjudications apply only if required by authorizing statute, the requirements of Sections 556 and 557 do not apply to a particular agency's rule-making activities unless Congress specifically demands it. As of 1985, Congress had done so only sixteen times.[27] Some are awfully important laws and

awfully important agencies, but not much of the federal government's rule making has to conform to the restrictions of these
particular sections of the APA.

The Administrative Procedure Act also governs the informal
rule-making process. Section 553 is silent on the question of ex-
parte contacts and such single party communications have become common practice in informal, that is to say nearly all,
agency rule making. The Section 556 requirement of a decision
on the record is replaced by the far looser "the agency shall
give interested persons an opportunity to participate in the rule
making through submission of written data, views, or arguments. . . . After consideration of the relevant matter presented,
the agency shall incorporate in the rules adopted a concise general statement of their basis and purpose" (553(c)). Letters, phone
calls, and informal face to face chats with clientele and professional and congressional supporters—those the agency feels
might possess "relevant matter"—can all be relied on even if no
one else has ever been told of their existence, let alone apprised of
their content and given the chance to present counterarguments.

There have been a couple of efforts to reduce the number and
the impact of ex-parte contacts, but neither has had all that
much effect. Executive Order 11920 instructs agency decision
makers not to discuss matters relating to the "disposition of rule
making proceedings" with any interested party, but only after
the notice of proposed rule making has been issued.[28] An awful
lot of contact can take place before that first notice is placed in the
Federal Register. A more sweeping effort to restrict ex-parte contacts was made by a panel of the U.S. Court for the District of
Columbia Circuit. In the case of *Home Box Office, Inc. v. FCC,*
the judges asked the Commission to produce a list of all single
party communications concerning its recently formulated pay-
cable rules. The list was sixty pages long, and, as Florence
Heffron noted, it "read like a Who's Who of Broadcasting."[29]
Appalled, the panel ruled that these contacts violated both Section 553 of the APA and the Government in the Sunshine Act.

But, later that same year, a second panel—of the same circuit—came to the opposite conclusion in the case of *Act v. FCC*.[30] The latter case was not appealed, and the Supreme Court denied certiorari in the HBO case, so it is a bit difficult to say exactly where we are. It does, however, look suspiciously like where we have been all along. To make rules agencies need information and ideas and they can and do routinely glean both from off the record communications with selected parties.

So where do we stand in our effort to reduce the bias so many of us believe is an inevitable by-product of allowing unrestricted ex-parte contacts? If Congress has concluded that the decisions—or in some cases just some of the decisions[31]—a particular agency is called upon to make should be "made on the record after opportunity for an agency hearing," then whether the decision is to be the judgment of a specific case or the promulgation of a general rule, the evidence to be relied on is very likely to have been scrutinized by everyone who managed to become a party to the decision. But most agencies operate and most decisions are reached in a far less restrictive environment. With loosely framed procedures they place on their own informal adjudications, and the near silence of the APA's Section 553, agency officials are free to contact—and be contacted by—anyone. The contacts are informal, off the record, and, in some cases, crucial ingredients in the final decision. Yet never are the parties forced to submit this information and those ideas to the scrutiny of those who might find them less than persuasive.

Ex-parte contacts leave the door to biased decision making wide open. Unfortunately, any effort to eliminate, or even restrict them, runs smack into two sizable obstacles. In the first place, it is impossible to impose any restrictions before the beginning of the notice and comment period. It is silly to suggest that an administrator could or should be required to recall every phone call, every letter, every personal visit that might have shaped his or her thinking about rules he or she has now come to see as needed. Should bureaucrats log and enter the editorials of the *New York*

Times or the long ago musings of a favorite graduate school professor? But, as noted earlier, if ex-parte contacts are only restricted during and after the notice and comment period, far too much has already been said and done for those restrictions to be very effective in reducing bias. Second, it is possible to outlaw ex-parte talking, but not ex-parte hearing. A bureaucrat, or any other professional for that matter, can be told he or she must hear this or read that, but not that he or she must take it seriously. So saying that the administrator cannot contact or be contacted unless it becomes part of a record that can be challenged may add to the flow of paper, but not of ideas. Still, if both contact and counterargument are included in some sort of record, reviewing agencies—especially courts—have a better chance to uncover bias and that is of some definite value.

IMPARTIAL DECISION MAKER

Bias can be present, of course, long before the first call from a congressional subcommittee Chair or the first letter from clientele group leaders. It can arise out of the desire for personal gain, the pull of ideology, or, probably more often than is recognized, the unshakable hold of professional commitment, but whatever its source, the most frightening kind of bias is the bias so strong that the evidence, collected selectively or not, appears to have no impact on the subsequent decision. To deal with that sort of bias we have tried to impose the requirement of an impartial decision maker.

The Goldberg Rules specifically state that an individual is entitled to have any decision bureaucracy makes made by an impartial decision maker and Verkuil found that thirty-eight of the forty-two programs he studied did in fact require it of themselves and tried to meet the requirement.[32] The rules for formal adjudications do not use the phrase "impartial decision maker" directly, but a number of provisions in Sections 554 and 556 of the Administrative Procedure Act are aimed at that result. Section 554 works to eliminate the bias that we all fear whenever the functions of prosecutor and judge are handled by a single individual. Any person who has been involved in either the investigation or the prosecution of a case may not "in that, or a factually related case, participate or advise in the decision . . . except as witness or counsel in public proceedings" (554(d)(2)). The very same section of the APA forbids assignment of the role of presiding officer/decision maker to anyone "responsible to or subject to the supervision or direction of an agency's investigative and/or prosecutorial staff." Finally, Section 556 dictates that the functions of presiding officers and decision makers be conducted in an impartial manner and leaves a fairly easy path out for an employee who feels he or she might be in any way biased (556(b)(3)). None of this guarantees impartiality, of course, but it helps to remind agency personnel of their legal and moral obligation to give everyone a fair shake and offers an avenue of appeal of the more obvious cases of bureaucratic bias and those are probably the best we can do and definitely worth doing.

Those engaged in formal rule making are subject to the Section 556 exhortation to function in an impartial manner and to disqualify themselves if they feel they cannot. Even that is missing from Section 553, but the courts have held that informal rule making, too, should be done by impartial decision makers.[33]

So, if the government wants to stop an individual's disability payments, decertify a stockyard, or produce a new rule governing noise levels in steel mills, the deed must be done by an impartial decision maker. But when is a decision maker impartial? In the context of Section 554 adjudications, at a minimum the person doing the judging has to be pretty far removed from those who do the prosecuting, but what about impartiality in rule making and informal adjudication? The answer is not entirely clear, but the courts have held the requirement of an impartial decision maker has been violated if it can be shown the official involved ignored an obvious conflict of interest or had clearly pre-judged the issue or case in question.

The U.S. Court of Appeals for the District of Columbia Circuit overturned a Federal Trade Commission decision involving the Cinderella Career and Finishing Schools, Inc., when it found that Commission Chairman Paul Rand Dixon had pre-judged the case against Cinderella, precluding any sort of fair disposition of the complaint.[34] The evidence was fairly clear—the Commissioner had given a speech denouncing something very close to the Cinderella actions while the case was pending—but just eight years later the D.C. Circuit held that then FTC Chairman Michael Pertschuk could participate in rule making concerning advertising on children's television programs despite the fact that he had been extremely active in condemning that advertising prior to the FTC announcement of its intent to draft a rule on the subject.[35] "Impartial," said the court, "does not mean uninformed, unthinking or inarticulate."[36]

In any case, pre-judgment has always been difficult to prove—suppose Mr. Dixon had written the speech prior to hearing the case but delivered it afterward—and the 1978 ruling on Chairman Pertschuk's alleged bias carries the standard of proof for disqualification on these grounds awfully far. In the words of the circuit judges, "An agency member may be disqualified from such a proceeding only when there is a clear and convincing showing that he has an unalterably closed mind on matters critical to the disposition of rule making."[37] In effect, one can do a good bit of preliminary deciding without being guilty of prejudgment. In defense of the courts and of hundreds of administrators, however, agencies generally don't suggest that rules are needed until a lot of preliminary investigation has taken place and some ideas have been kicked around. Anyone who emerges from that sort of process with a completely open mind may have come out with a completely empty one as well.

It can be pretty difficult to remain an impartial decision maker when one stands to gain or lose depending upon the outcome of the decision. The courts have consistently held that officials must not make decisions when confronted by such conflicts of interest and there are statutes and executive orders trying to make sure they don't.[38] The problem seldom occurs in formal adjudication because of extensive reliance on Administrative Law Judges, and one doubts it is widespread in informal adjudication either. But rule making could be different. A lot of rules must be approved by political appointees—the regulatory commissioners are all appointees and even OSHA rules must get by the Secretary of Labor—and many of these men and women have substantial financial holdings. The potential for financial conflict of interest is always there, but I don't believe it is tapped all that often at this top level. Short tenure in office, blind trusts, media bloodhounds (if someone else smells the blood first), and even a dose of honesty and commitment to public service, all work against it.

But there is another, more subtle conflict of interest that can afflict these political appointees and, more to the point, the extremely important career staff below. Given the pattern of appointments to top-level bureaucratic positions discussed earlier, there are ties between these people and the industries who will be subject to their rules besides the opportunity for the former to make another buck. Career staff, too, have a powerful feeling of empathy toward these "outsiders." There is no personal gain in the traditional legal sense, just a pull toward one set of people and interests, but it is a pull that is hard to resist.

The law and the courts have made an effort to reduce bias in bureaucratic decision making. The people who make the decisions are expected to be impartial and to collect evidence in an open and aboveboard manner, giving all interested parties a real chance to evaluate and even to challenge that evidence before a decision is finally reached.

Formal adjudications, governed by Sections 554, 556, and 557 of the Administrative Procedure Act, are handled in precisely that fashion. Informal adjudications are handled pretty much the way the agency wants to, with the Goldberg Rules providing a set of guidelines, but not a set of hard and fast procedures. When it comes to judging specific cases, the federal government on occasion can be arbitrary, irrational, and unfair, but it is not systematically biased.

Rule making, on the other hand, is a very different game. Procedural requirements for formal rule making are stringent, particularly Section 557(d)(1)(A)−(E) on ex-parte contacts, but the impartial decision maker requirement is weak even here, and, in any case, very few rules end up being made this way. Most are made informally, subject only to the requirements of Section 553 and subsequent court cases, and both the Congress and the courts have left plenty of room for bureaucracy's natural bias.

Pre-judgment seems to mean bias etched in stone—and dated—and conflict of interest the prospect of personal gain. As a practical matter, if all the agency personnel who define the public interest in terms of the interests of their supporters were disqualified for conflict of interest there would hardly be anyone left to do the deciding. Still, these are not really impartial decision makers.

Even more importantly, the almost unrestricted flow of ex-parte communications frequently builds a record to defend a decision, not to make one. All too often, the convinced talk to the convinced, with never so much as a skeptic, let alone a heretic, allowed in on the conversation. Again, as a practical matter, we cannot cut off communication between agencies and the people who care so much about what these agencies are doing. But, because so much of that communication is one sided, if unchallenged it is bound to lead to bias, and so very often it remains unchallenged because those who would challenge it have no idea it has taken place.

In short, the courts and the APA try to reduce bureaucratic bias by requiring that decisions be made by impartial decision makers and restricting ex-parte contacts. Both work to some extent in the realm of adjudication and the latter has some impact on formal rule making as well. But, in the crucial arena of informal rule making, neither has much effect. Bureaucrats with powerful ties to their support groups can keep the communications channels open, hear selectively, and decide with a clear conscience. To them, agency policy making as usual is unbiased and most of the time the courts agree.

Opening the System

Bureaucrats tend to have a fairly restrictive view of who ought to participate in agency deliberations and influence agency decisions. In addition, there is the strong suspicion that most agencies prefer to do their business as far from the public eye as possible. I am not all that convinced that bureaucrats are any more allergic to the "sunshine" than are legislators, chief executives, or judges, but be that as it may, the APA and the courts have attempted to force bureaucracy to do more of its work in public and to allow more people more opportunities for more effective participation in the policy process.

These efforts have centered on three primary concerns. First, notice: that is, we want to be certain that people know when and where decisions that will affect their interests will be made. Second, opportunity: that is, we want to know that those who feel they will be affected by a decision have had a chance to tell the decision makers what they feel should be done and why. Finally, accountability—we want all of this done in public with a careful and detailed record of what was done, how it was done, and why it was done.

NOTICE

The Administrative Procedure Act does require that agencies make public their intent to take any sort of action, but, as usual, the type of notice required varies. Whether the final action will be in the form of a general rule or the adjudication of a specific case, if that particular action is "required by statute to be determined on the record after opportunity for an agency hearing" (Sec. 554(a)), the agency must provide to "persons entitled to notice" information concerning, "(1) the time, place, and nature of the hearing; (2) the legal authority and jurisdiction under which the hearing is to be held; and (3) the matters of fact and law asserted" (Sec. 554(b)). If, on the other hand, an agency is engaged in informal (Sec. 553) rule making, the requirement is for a general notice to be published in the Federal Register. The notice must include "(1) a statement of the time, place, and nature of public rule making proceedings; (2) reference to the legal authority under which the rule is proposed; and (3) either the terms or substance of the proposed rule or a description of the subjects and issues involved" (Sec. 553(b)). Finally, as usual, informal adjudications have a hodgepodge of restrictions imposed by the courts or the agencies themselves.

As Paul Verkuil makes clear, informal adjudication almost always follows "timely and adequate notice." Specifically, forty of the forty-two programs he examined imposed such a requirement on themselves.[39] The two remaining had no designated procedures at all, but still one somehow doubts that even these bureaucrats routinely made decisions affecting other people's lives without so much as telling them what was happening.

Notice requirements for actions taken after opportunity for an agency hearing are clear as can be concerning what is to be said, but painfully silent on the question of to whom the agency must say it. If the action is adjudicatory in nature, the party or parties named in the action are clearly entitled, but beyond that whom to notify seems to be a matter for each agency to decide for itself.[40] In formal rule making, the agency is even more on its own, since there is no party named in the action. Agencies are good about providing notice to those they believe have something to contribute, but not all that many have gone much beyond that comfortable circle except, perhaps, to notify their very vocal critics in order to cut off one avenue of appeal to the courts.

Finally, informal rule making can be done after general notice in the *Federal Register*. The notice must contain some fairly important information—enough to mount a pretty good challenge if you know what you are doing—but how many people will actually see it and who will they be? The *Register* is essential reading for all informed lobbyists—including those for critical and public interest groups—and probably for some congressional staffers as well, though in most cases all of the above already will have heard. When it comes to the rest of us, however, the utility of the *Federal Register* in keeping us abreast of the latest in government was clearly stated by Justice Hugo Black in his dissent in *Federal Crop Insurance Corporation v. Merrill*: "To my mind it is an absurdity to hold that every farmer who insures his crops knows what the Federal Register contains or even knows that there is such a publication. If he were to peruse this voluminous and dull publication as it is issued from time to time in order to make sure whether anything has been promulgated that affects his rights, he would never need crop insurance, for he would never get time to plant any crops. Nor am I convinced that a reading of technically-worded regulations would enlighten him much in any event."[41]

So there are notification requirements, but outside of their considerable utility in protecting specific individuals threatened with adverse adjudicatory actions by executive branch agencies, the requirements don't spread information about agency activity much farther than it would have gone in any case. Clientele, professional, and congressional supporters are bound to know what their agencies are up to. It is part of the informal give and take that is such an important part of their ongoing relationship. Notice requirements have probably helped critics keep a foot in the door and that is of some value. But, by and large, telling bureaucrats that they must notify the public of what they plan to do has little effect on either the planning or the doing.

OPPORTUNITY

Section 553 of the Administrative Procedure Act requires agencies to "give interested persons an opportunity to participate in the rule making through submission of written data, views, or arguments." When rule making turns formal, Section 556(d) states that any "party is entitled to present his case or defense by oral or documentary evidence, to submit rebuttal evidence, and to conduct such cross-examination as may be required for a full and true disclosure of the facts." Formal adjudications are conducted under the same set of rules as formal rule making, and, once again, informal adjudication is pretty much up to the agency unless the courts have spoken about its particular programs. Paul Verkuil found that only about half of the programs he examined included the requirement of an opportunity to present "the other side" of the case.[42]

The law requires that agencies let people speak to the issues and questions these agencies are about to decide. The courts have prodded agencies that seemed reluctant to do so and occasionally even forced an expansion of the list of those entitled to be heard.[43] Still, two powerful forces are at work to undermine the impact these procedural requirements might have on bureaucratic decision making.

First of all, the opportunity to participate is not going to be spread any farther than the notice of what is to be decided, when, and where. That isn't very far, and, more to the point, it isn't very far outside an agency's normal set of supporters. Some critics are going to get in and that's important, but as I have argued time and again, that is not enough to move bureaucrats far from their traditional path.

Second, and even more to the point, the opportunity to speak is important, but it is the opportunity to be heard and taken seriously we are really after, and the APA and the courts can't quite make that guarantee. Informal rule making still leaves far too much room for ex-parte contacts, and agency careerists, steeped in a sincere conviction that they are being both competent and responsible, hear mostly what they want to hear.

I do not mean to say that the APA requirements and court decisions that guarantee to the public opportunities to participate in agency policy making are meaningless. Many of the most determined critics are now routine participants in agency decision making, and some of what they say is heard. Even if it isn't, it may find its way into the public record or become the basis for a subsequent legal challenge. Important as such developments may be, they have left most agencies with nothing worse than a thorn in the side, and, as I argued in the previous chapter, a sometimes useful thorn at that. The requirement to let the public speak does not produce a major change in bureaucratic policy making.

ACCOUNTABILITY

Finally comes accountability—the requirement that decision makers build a careful and detailed public record that tells us what was decided, how it was decided, and why it came out the way it did. This is the most important requirement of all, for as much as all of us may lament it, most agencies could take out full-page ads in every newspaper in the country and still not broaden the audience of interested parties much. Besides, professionals will always balk at following the lead of amateurs. Notice and opportunity are important and worthy objectives, but almost impossible to reach. Accountability may not be. If there is a detailed public record, there can be a detailed public review. The courts, the Congress, and the President can evaluate decisions on substantive, procedural, even on political grounds and move to change things they don't like. I realize that this is after the fact and that, from all I have said in the past few chapters, Congress is pretty much satisfied with bureaucratic decision making as is and the President and the courts can't do too much about it. But a clear public record gives the President and the courts a chance for influence, and there is a good probability that record will find its way to members of Congress other than those already a part of a comfortable agency-subcommittee alliance. In addition, knowing such a record will be available for review may cause individual bureaucrats to consider their judgments more carefully and even to temper their biases. A requirement of accountability won't produce miracles, but of the three procedural rules aimed at making the bureaucratic decision-making system more open and inclusive, it has by far the best chance of success.

For both formal adjudication and formal rule making, the record an agency must build is formidable. The agency is given the authority to exclude "irrelevant, immaterial or unduly repetitious evidence" (Sec. 556(d)), but the record is still going to be a very complete one and the law makes this record the exclusive basis for the decision to be reached. Should anyone wish to review such a decision, there is a pile of documents and an administrator who knows he or she must be able to use that pile to show how and why this particular decision was reached. If courts do the reviewing, they must do it within the confines of Section 706 of the Administrative Procedure Act, including the important, if fuzzy, substantial evidence test, but if Congress or the President decides to look things over there really aren't any rules. Presidential review isn't too likely, and it is usually the "right" members of Congress who end up looking to see if they are satisfied. But the record is so public that it is hard to be sure it will stay in friendly hands and a disappointed interested party— with enough money—can mount a challenge in court. Traditional agency supporters won't have to take a back seat, but they may have to share the bus for a change.

In stark contrast, Section 553 merely requires that agencies "incorporate in the rules adopted a concise general statement of their basis and purpose." Again, should the Congress or the President want to do a little digging, the question of what sort of record bureaucrats need to be able to produce is irrelevant. Not so for the courts, however, and they have an extremely difficult time deciding just what sort of record is required and when an agency action can be set aside as "arbitrary and capricious, an abuse of discretion" (Sec. 706(2)(A)). In 1975 the U.S. Supreme Court determined that court review "should be confined to examination of the 'reasons' statement, and the determination whether the statement, *without more*, evinces that the Secretary's decision is so irrational as to constitute the decision arbitrary and capricious."[44] A year later the D.C. Circuit Court of Appeals went along with looking at the "reasons statement," but hastened to add that "the 'basis and purpose' statement . . . must be sufficiently detailed and informative to allow a *searching judicial scrutiny* of how and why the regulations were adopted."[45] As noted earlier, Mr. Justice Rehnquist tried to chide the rest of the federal courts for such aggressiveness in his opinion in the *Vermont Yankee* case, but the swirling legal battle of the on again—off again air bag rule suggests he did not reach all of them. So the water is muddy, but we do know this much. The record required is far less extensive and the burden of proof a lot easier to bear.

The Administrative Procedure Act constitutes a serious effort to make the bureaucratic decision-making process more open and inclusive. Agencies are instructed to notify the public, or at least the directly affected segments of it, of decisions to be made, give these people an opportunity to provide information and arguments relevant to the issues involved, and construct a record of what was done along with how and why it was done so that other governmental institutions may evaluate their decisions. The courts have had their say as well, telling the FCC that the viewing audience was an interested party in license proceedings, the Bureau of Indian Affairs that its staff manual could not serve as a set of binding substantive rules, and HEW that the basis and purpose statement required for 553 rule making had to give a pretty clear picture of how and why the rule was adopted.[46]

But, in the end, all of this has a limited impact on bureaucratic decision making. Notice seldom goes beyond an agency's normal supporters, and when it does it gets to a handful of by now almost traditional critics. Opportunity, too, is limited and almost always to the same set of individuals and groups. Without notice there is no opportunity, and selective hearing mitigates the impact of anything said by outsiders. Finally, there is the public record. For some decisions it must be detailed and extensive and the decision must be supported by substantial evidence in that record. For the rest, however, the record is a "concise statement of

basis and purpose" and there is still a good bit of judicial dis-
agreement about how detailed that statement must be. On top of
that, the grounds for setting aside actions covered by Section 553
procedures is the infamous "arbitrary and capricious" and if all
federal judges fall in line behind the Supreme Court of the last
decade, there is going to be an awful lot of room for administrative discretion. It is hard to see how a basis and purpose statement could be poorly enough drafted that "the statement, without more, evinces that the Secretary's decision is so irrational as
to constitute the decision arbitrary and capricious." [47] There are
rules, and the rules have guaranteed critics a place at the table,
but despite the definite value of having them there, that presence
alone is not enough to have a substantial effect on bureaucracy.

Summary and Conclusion

Most bureaucratic decisions are never reviewed in court. Some
can't be, but most just aren't challenged. No one has the combination of anger, patience, and dollars such a challenge requires.
As long as most decisions go uncontested, the courts will never
be a pervasive influence in bureaucratic policy making. Still, it
would be a mistake to underestimate the impact that judges can,
and do, have on what happens in the executive branch.

In the first place, court decisions speak to the future as well as
the past. They tell agencies whether they did the right thing in
this case, but also how to act in similar situations later on. It
is true that this guidance can be less than clear and precise —
how should a college admissions officer react to the *Bakke* decision — but court decisions do offer some idea of where to go and
bureaucrats will generally try to live within them.

Even more important is the fact that there is some truth to the
assertion that, even though the courts don't review many bureaucratic decisions, they do review many of the important ones. The
courts don't look at every single decision to terminate welfare
benefits, but they did look at the question of whether or not

such terminations could take place without providing the individual recipient a hearing *before* the payments were stopped. The Supreme Court's answer was No.

So court influence is not pervasive, and it is a far cry from systematic—lots of people, including OSHA's own staff, have a hard time figuring out why the benzene rule lost when the cotton dust rule won—but it is important. A single decision can wipe out years of agency activity, or save them. But, by definition, these court decisions are agency specific, or, more properly, agency and decision specific—again, remember the benzene rule lost, but the cotton dust rule won—so it is virtually impossible to draw any general conclusions about court influence. About all we can say is that there is some, sometimes a lot.

Since it is all but impossible to paint a coherent picture of the scope and nature of court influence over bureaucracy, prospects for a quick and easy answer to the question of whether or not court influence advances democratic values are bleak indeed. Even if we agree that the crucial job we assign to the courts in reviewing administrative decision making is to strike a proper balance between the majority's legitimate interests/objectives— as reflected in legislative and executive action—and the individual's right to be free from unwarranted and obtrusive government intrusion into his or her life—as reflected in the rights guaranteed by the U.S. Constitution—it is almost impossible to give those courts a grade that is anything but subjective. The Supreme Court said that welfare benefits cannot be cut off without a pre-termination hearing (*Goldberg v. Kelly*). Disability payments made under the Social Security Act can be (*Mathews v. Eldridge*). Does one of these represent a proper balance? Which one? How about both? That's what Mr. Justice White thought. Other examples abound. A high school student suspended for disciplinary reasons is entitled to a hearing beforehand (*Goss v. Lopez*), but a medical student bounced for "poor clinical performance and lack of attention to personal hygiene" is not (*Missouri v. Horowitz*). Whether the court strikes the proper balance between the individual and the majority is a matter of opinion, those opinions flow from deeply held values, and we have puzzled over the question from the earliest days of the nation.

Then there are the rules. The rules, too, vary from one agency to another, and even within the same agency can vary from one type of decision to another. Still, when compared to that of court decisions, the impact of the rules seems almost straightforward and systematic. The rules are supposed to reduce bureaucratic bias and make the decision-making system more open and accountable. They do. Sort of.

Rules to reduce bias guarantee an impartial decision maker and try to eliminate ex-parte contacts. The impartial decision-maker rule goes after two of the worst sources of bias—a mind already made up or a person with some economic stake in the outcome—but leaves far more subtle types of bias alone. What about the bias toward support groups that comes from years of working together, or the blinders that come with a passionate commitment to one side or the other in a clash of ideas within a particular segment of the scientific community? Couldn't these cause bias? In fairness, there may be no way to write rules to eliminate this kind of bias, but we are left a ways short of the promise of an impartial decision maker. Likewise, ex-parte contacts—on the talking side anyway—are pretty well driven out of formal rule making and formal adjudication, and aren't all that prevalent in informal adjudication either. But such contacts are a way of life in informal rule making, and, in any event, the listening side of any contact with bureaucracy is almost certainly beyond the rules. How can you force anyone to take a letter, memo, or phone call seriously? You can tell someone to log it, put it in the record—if there is one—even to show it to all interested parties, but you can't force someone to believe its contents. Ex-parte hearing is not just something your grandfather does to your grandmother (or vice-versa) after fifty years together. We all do it.

We want to open the system and requirements of notice and opportunity have pushed in that direction. Despite my obvious admiration for Mr. Justice Black's comments on the *Federal*

Register, we have probably opened the system to about as many people as have any serious desire to come in. The general public simply doesn't have the incentive, or the capacity, to organize itself for a serious onslaught on some agency about to write a rule, and in my darker moments I sometimes wonder what contribution that public would make if it ever did.

So we come to the paper trail. Bureaucrats have to leave a record, a record that tells us what they did, why they did it, and how they did it. For some decisions that record is extensive, and it alone is supposed to be the basis of the decision. If asked, a judge can look at that record and cause all sorts of trouble if he or she doesn't like the looks of it. That has to have some impact on a bureaucrat about to decide something, but given what I said a couple of pages ago about the idiosyncratic nature of court decisions, it is awfully hard to say just what that impact is. I suspect it is to make sure everything is done within whatever rules are supposed to apply. For other decisions, however, the record to be compiled is pretty sketchy, for others yet, virtually non-existent. It is hard to imagine the "statement of basis and purpose" requirement having much of an impact on agency decision making. It's a piece of paper to be filed, but not a whole lot more in most cases.

Is the system more open? Yes, in one significant sense it is. Rules demanding notice and opportunity have helped to give bureaucracy's critics a place at the table. Not even James Watt could force the Sierra Club out. The courts would never have allowed it. As I said in the previous chapter, bureaucrats and their critics have now reached a mutually beneficial, if somewhat tense, accommodation and, except for the occasional true believer like Watt, have no real desire to throw their critics out the door. But the rules of administrative law and the decisions of the courts brought them in in the first place. The value of having them there is still a matter for considerable debate, but they are there to stay, and that much, if nothing else, we can credit to the rules.

CONCLUSION

B ureaucrats don't make policy on their own. They couldn't even if they wanted to, but they don't really want to. They are quite comfortable with their role of partner—senior partner to be sure, but partner—in a cooperative policy-making enterprise. This particular co-op isn't open to everybody, of course, but if you have the requisite combination of specialized knowledge and political power, bureaucrats will make room.

Congressional subcommittees have plenty of both, and no agency would give serious thought to trying to make policy without including key members and staff from the appropriate subcommittees in the deliberations. Likewise, clientele groups, professional associations, and a few individual policy experts have a lot of one and enough of the other to make them accept-able, and useful, partners. All of this adds up to considerable influence over agency decision making, but I suspect that inter-action among these people is so common and their view of the world so similar that neither side sees it as influence. It's more like "putting our heads together" to find the right answer. And everyone involved sees it as so natural. At 6:55 this morning (May 12, 1986) WFHR's Ag Watch News concluded with the announce-ment that the Agriculture Department and the National Cattle-man's Association had settled on a plan for implementation of the Whole Herd Buyout Plan for dairy farmers. Not once did the reporter use the word influence.

Critics are not partners. For all of the reasons outlined in Chapter 4, they don't want to be. They do want to be participants, however, and they generally are. The rules of administrative law allowed them to get their foot (feet?) in the door, but both the critics and the agencies came to realize that if said feet stayed in the door—nothing more, mind you, just the feet—it would be good for both sides. So critics have some influence and they tend to use it to push for decisions almost certain to be unpopular with the normal supporters of whatever agency is being pushed. Overall an agency's critics can scarcely be considered serious competitors with its supporters, but on any particular decision they can be powerful policy makers indeed.

Judges aren't partners either. Partnership may well be beneath their judicial dignity anyway, but since the courts divide up the turf on a geographic basis and not a policy one, there is no way that judges could pass the knowledge test for admission even should they want to. Work loads and lack of expertise keep judges from even being regular participants, but when they do get in they can stand everything on its head. OSHA was fiercely committed to its 1 ppm benzene rule and the evidence linking benzene and leukemia dates back to the 1920's, but the Supreme Court said No and five years of work came to nothing. Like bureaucratic critics, judges are not a consistently powerful force in the decision-making world of any agency, but when their influence is felt, it is really felt.

Finally, the President is neither partner or participant. Nobody wants him to be, at least not on anything that would approach a regular basis. But he is President. That means that when he decides it is time to get in on the act, he expects to be more than partner or participant. He expects to be boss. In some situations he is; in others he's not. Which ones are which has already been discussed at length in Chapter 2, so all that should be needed here is to remind you that a President who wants to slow or stop something has all the knowledge and most of the power he needs to be boss. A President who wants to chart a new direction or put an agency on fast forward is going to be hard pressed to get even participant status.

Bureaucracy and the General Public Interest

As noted time and again throughout the book, agencies and their supporters have a very narrow—and self-interested—concept of the public interest and they will pursue it with single-minded dedication. Critics can force them off this path. So can Presidents. Even judges can do it. They can be forced to make a different decision, all right, but not to adopt a different definition of the public interest. That's too thoroughly ingrained, too comforting, too convincing to be susceptible to assault. So critics, Presidents, and judges win some, but supporters win the rest, including all the little seemingly automatic ones that end up giving real meaning to a particular policy.

Obviously none of this comes as any real surprise to anyone. The seed was first planted in my own mind by Roscoe Martin and Emmette Redford in a course they taught to aspiring MPA candidates at Syracuse University in the summer of 1965. Arthur Maass wrote about it long before that.[1] It even finds its way into American government textbooks and syndicated columns.

Special interest politics is seen as the primary culprit in all of this and it is clear that it does play an important role. Clientele group backing and the sympathetic ear for group demands that goes with it have become a bureaucratic, not just a congressional, way of life. But it is easy to overestimate the importance of special interest politics. Bureaucrats are politicians, generally very good ones, but they are also human beings, and, more to the point, they are policy experts. Over the long run, what they do has to pass personal and technical as well as political muster. Consider the case of the Bureau of Reclamation and the effort to turn the Interior West from desert to farmland.

The Reclamation Act of 1902 placed a limit of 160 acres (320 for husband and wife) on the amount of land that could be owned and irrigated with water from federal water projects and required that a farmer live "in the neighborhood" of his farm to be eligible to purchase the water from the federally built irrigation systems. The purpose of these provisions, forcefully articulated on the floor of Congress by the Act's chief sponsor, Nevada Democrat Francis G. Newlands, was "to guard against land monopoly and to hold this land in small tracts for the people of the entire country, to give to each only the amount of land that will be necessary for the support of a family."[2] The Bureau proceeded to define "in the neighborhood" as within fifty miles of the farm—this is 1910 Colorado, not 1986 California—and ignored the acreage limitations altogether.

Congress amended reclamation law in 1926, allowing a farmer to own and irrigate "excess land" (more than the allowable 160 or 320) provided that he or she signed a *recordable contract* with the Bureau of Reclamation. In that contract, the farmer agreed to sell that excess land at the *dry land price* (a fraction of its value when irrigated) ten years after the date of the contract signing. Congress hoped that such a provision would bring more land into cultivation quickly, but then bring that land back onto the market at a reasonable price for new generations. The 1926 law did not restate the residency requirement, though it was never clear whether this was deliberate or merely an oversight. In any case, the Bureau dropped even the generous fifty-mile requirement and signed recordable contracts with everyone who owned more than the law allowed—signed them, but never enforced them.

Finally, 1939 saw one more revision of reclamation law, this time granting each farmer a ten-year "development" period—no payments on a project—and allowing forty years to pay back project costs. The interest rate was zero percent. In addition, for the first time, the Bureau was allowed to charge part—up to 80 percent—of the cost of an irrigation project to "other beneficiaries." Water skiers, boaters, and most of all hydroelectric customers, now began to pay for most of the dams.

In the meantime, the 1902 act had allowed farmers to irrigate leased land, providing the residency requirement was met. With that requirement defined out of existence, those who could find the money discovered they could lease land in different parts of the West with different growing seasons. All that was needed was money, managers, and plenty of migrant labor, and the Southern Pacific Land Company, among others, could get its hands on all three.

By the time the Bureau was all done, the Interior West was an agricultural region, but Representative Newlands would never have recognized it. In 1979, there were over 2 million acres of "excess land" being irrigated and the two largest reclamation land "farmers" — 100,000 plus acres each — were two wholly owned subsidiaries of the Southern Pacific Railroad. Tenneco, Chevron, Superior, and Getty Oil were all in the farming business, along with fertilizer manufacturers, and even a couple of 25,000– 30,000-acre operations owned by folks whose sole business is agriculture. Subsidies to these "family farms" run in the vicinity of $1,500 per acre and the resulting dollar total is so staggering it caused California Representative George Miller (D.) to label it "the biggest Western stage coach robbery of the public since Jesse James."[3]

Reclamation land "farmers" include some wealthy individuals and some powerful corporations. Their power, expressing itself in all of the usual ways, played a role in the creation of this system. But, in the minds of Bureau of Reclamation personnel, each of the key decisions that produced the system made perfectly good personal and professional sense. On a personal level, these were Westerners. A region of small family farms may make sense to someone from Iowa, but it is almost laughable to someone from Montana. People born in Colorado, California, or Idaho don't see much sense in it either. And, most important of all, these decisions helped to accomplish the Bureau's three key goals: cultivate as much land as possible, cultivate it as quickly as possible, and keep reclamation land food prices competitive.

By the time the first reclamation law passed there were already some large farming operations in existence, and more than a few were absentee operations. There seemed no compelling reason to force these people out of business or reduce the value of their land, and ignoring residency requirements and acreage limitations not only was a way to leave well enough alone, but had the added effect of bringing lots of land into cultivation quickly. Once the projects were completed it seemed a little silly to Bureau personnel to let land lie idle while they waited for someone to come along to buy 160 acres of it and get going. This became a particularly acute problem in the 1920's and 1930's, when so few people could pay even the dry land price for what was available. If wealthy Easterners, the Southern Pacific Railroad, or a local farmer who already owned a thousand acres had the money to put another thousand or two into cultivation, why quibble? Wasn't it better to see the water used and the land produce than to stick to the letter of the law—a law they didn't have much use for anyway—and waste the resources of "their" land?

The same sort of rationale applied to non-enforcement of recordable contracts, unlimited leasing by non-residents, and the allocation of costs among project beneficiaries. A farmer cannot sell excess land when there are no buyers, and to deny the water at that point would be to pull land out of production. Unlimited leasing allowed "farmers" to cultivate land with different growing seasons. With some careful planning and a little luck, a lettuce grower could market fresh lettuce for four to six months rather than four to six weeks. Finally, the more of a reclamation project's cost that can be passed on to power customers or other beneficiaries, the lower the price of food produced on reclamation land. Western farmers have to recover the costs of their water. The economic difference between paying the full cost of a project and paying one quarter of that cost requires no further explanation. Besides, hydroelectric customers do benefit, it is only a few extra pennies per kilowatt hour, and, even with these costs added, it is difficult to find cheaper electricity anywhere in the country.

To an outside observer, all of this may seem like nothing more than rationalization for policies pursued to enhance clientele interests. But Bureau personnel rarely talked to outside observers, and outsider is just another word for amateur anyway, so how could that outsider understand? Besides, the Bureau and its supporters had all the proof they needed. Millions of acres that once lay idle now produced everything from wheat and soybeans to lettuce and watermelons, fresh produce was available for much of the year, and Americans were paying less for food than almost any other people.

I do not mean to endorse the wisdom or fairness of federal reclamation policy. We almost certainly could have turned that land from snakes and sagebrush to corn and tomatoes without an inverse redistribution of income of this magnitude. Jesse James generally stuck to trains and banks. Otherwise Representative Miller is probably right. But Bureau of Reclamation personnel don't think so. They do believe that these policies were just as sound technically as they were politically, and I believe that the vast majority of bureaucrats feel the same way about almost all of what they do.

Bureaucracy and Competent Policy

If outside influence doesn't lead to the introduction of majoritarian influences, maybe we can take some comfort in the fact that at least it doesn't lead us away from the goal of competent (effective) public policy. After all, there has always been some fear that too much influence by the public, especially the general public, would make it impossible for the "experts" to use their knowledge to make sound and workable policy. Indeed, as Francis Rourke has pointed out, there is a long tradition among scholars of bureaucracy lamenting the fact that "the criteria of responsiveness and effectiveness often point in opposite directions."[4] Since the outsiders who do influence agency decision making are generally experts themselves, at least we ought to avoid the incompetence trap.

No such luck. In what may be the ultimate irony of contemporary bureaucracy, the very fact that all of these outsiders are from the same specialized "issue network" as the bureaucrats they seek to influence reinforces the incompetence that all too often is the by-product of the narrowness and parochialism of the committed professional. To borrow a piece of eloquent imagery from Frederick Mosher: "Except for those few professionals who grow beyond their field, the real world is seen as by a submariner through a periscope whose direction and focus are fixed."[5] Such submariners can indeed see where they are going, but not where they might have gone instead. To an engineer, a well-designed bridge is a thing of beauty. It represents a triumph of skill and knowledge—his or her skill and knowledge—and it is easy to become so immersed in the process of building the dam that the question of whether or not it should be built is lost in the shuffle of blueprints and plans.

The very same thing can happen to any professional and the possible consequences are neatly summarized by Hugh Heclo. "It is not difficult to imagine situations in which policies make excellent sense within the cloisters of the expert issue watchers and yet are nonsense or worse seen from the viewpoint of ordinary people, the kinds of people political executives rarely meet."[6]

Heclo's comments might have been written to serve as the epitaph for the first three decades of the Federal Housing Administration. During that first thirty years, the FHA guaranteed more than $110 billion in home mortgages. Very early in its existence the agency committed itself to sound banking principles as the guide for its mortgage guarantee policy; that is, agency success would be judged "by the number of loans made and the repayment record."[7] Concern for the "repayment record" led the FHA to search for the best (least risky) loans it could find and it did not take long for these real estate—banking industry experts to conclude that new, single family, owner-occupied housing was the

answer to their professional dreams. So, from the 1930's to the
late 1960's, that is where the agency put its (our) $110 billion
worth of guarantees.

As Harold Seidman points out, these policies make perfectly
good sense, "if a remarkably low default rate were the sole criterion of program effectiveness."[8] To the men and women who
ran the agency this was the sole criterion and they were satisfied,
but if we take a broader perspective, it is clear that the FHA's
single-minded pursuit of its notion of competent and responsible
policy was anything but.

In the first place, the only land available for the large-scale
construction of new single family dwellings was located outside
the nation's cities. As a result, the lower interest rates on FHA
guaranteed mortgages coupled with the minimal down payments required for "qualified buyers" constituted a considerable
subsidy to the creation of suburbia. FHA guarantees for the purchase and renovation of inner city housing might not have
stemmed the tide of suburban growth, and a lot of other forces
were at work in the process of ringing our cities with hundreds
of satellite communities and miles and miles of highways. Still,
FHA policies were a definite contributor and the narrow professional perspective of the agency's personnel kept them from
recognizing that contribution.

Second, there can be little doubt that FHA policies helped
to perpetuate segregated residential patterns and to exacerbate
the housing problems of lower- and middle-class Blacks in our
major cities. Even those Blacks who could afford the types of
houses available in FHA-preferred suburbs faced tremendous
social and psychological, not to mention legal, barriers to relo-
cation. Not everyone is a Jackie Robinson. For most it was stay
behind, but there were no FHA guarantees for older housing
inside the city. Further, there were no guarantees for rental housing, so most Blacks, who were renters, saw the deterioration
of their neighborhoods accelerated as lenders put their money
where the federal government would guarantee its repayment.
Finally, there was evidence that by the 1960's the FHA condoned,

in some cases actively participated with banks and insurance companies in, the writing off of entire areas of large cities. With red lines on city maps and an unwillingness to lend or insure within the lines, some parts of our largest cities were left to die.[9]

No one at the Federal Housing Administration set out to create a sprawling, ugly city choking on its own exhaust, nor to condemn Blacks to poor housing in what remained of our central cities. Indeed, the ultimate irony of all of this is the fact that there were almost certainly FHA professionals who condemned these developments even as their policies contributed to them. Through the filter of the banker–real estate perspective of these professionals, these developments were a shame, their policies a triumph, and the two totally unrelated.

The process of specialization itself is based on narrowing the range of questions one confronts so that the amount and range of knowledge needed to answer those questions becomes manageable. Consequently, there is little prospect for escape from this sort of professional narrowness and isolation. Fortunately, we do not need a complete escape. If the nation needs a workable plan for its national forests, that plan will not emerge from a room from which all professional foresters have been summarily banned. Neither will it emerge from a room into which only professional foresters have been admitted. The narrow perspective of the forester is vital. The danger comes when that narrow perspective is the only one brought to bear, for, as Harold Laski argued over half a century ago, that perspective inevitably comes to "mistake its technical results for social wisdom."[10] When that happens even the most knowledgeable of experts becomes a threat to competent public policy.

A Final Word

The executive branch of the federal government is a loose collection of narrowly focused and highly specialized agencies. Each has its own view of the proper shape and direction for policy in its own domain, and though all are subject to outside influence, most of the time that influence serves as a powerful reinforcement for bureaucracy's own view of where it ought to be going. There are exceptions, but they are just that, exceptions.

Unfortunately, two rather important political values — concern for a general public interest and competence — can easily be casualties of this highly professionalized, agency-centered policy-making process. Neither is a deliberate casualty, at least not in the sense that agency careerists set out to produce incompetent policies at odds with the interests and/or preferences of a majority of citizens. When competence is lost, it is lost to the isolation and narrowness of Mosher's "fixed-focus submariner." When the general public interest is submerged, it is submerged not so much by the greed of "the special interests" as by the sincere bureaucratic conviction that these are the only sound and workable — that is, expert generated — policies around and the blinders that keep experts from seeing the forest, even as they count and categorize the trees.

In sum, in a fundamental sense, the contemporary federal bureaucracy is irresponsible. But since its irresponsibility is based as much or more on sincere conviction as on self-interest, and because it is draped in the trappings of specialized knowledge, not political power, it is so much harder to see, so much harder to understand, and ever so much harder to combat.

Notes

Chapter 1

1. Carl J. Friedrich, "Public Policy and the Nature of Administrative Responsibility," *Public Policy* 1 (1940): 3–24, and John M. Gaus, "The Responsibility of Public Administration," in John M. Gaus, Leonard D. White, and Marshall E. Dimock, *The Frontiers of Public Administration* (Chicago: University of Chicago Press, 1936), pp. 26–45, esp. pp. 39–40. The most readily accessible version of Friedrich's article—and the one I used—is found in Francis E. Rourke, ed., *Bureaucratic Power in National Politics* (3rd ed.; Boston: Little, Brown and Co., 1978), pp. 399–409.

2. Francis E. Rourke, *Bureaucracy, Politics, and Public Policy* (3rd ed.; Boston: Little, Brown and Co., 1984), p. 205. In the first edition (1969) it appeared on p. 145, and in the second (1976) on p. 177.

3. Herman Finer, "Administrative Responsibility in Democratic Government," *Public Administration Review* 2 (Summer 1941): 335–350. Again, the most accessible version is found in Rourke, ed., *Bureaucratic Power*, pp. 410–421, which I shall cite hereafter.

4. *Ibid.*, p. 412.

5. Arthur Maass, *Muddy Waters: The Army Engineers and the Nation's Rivers* (Cambridge, Mass.: Harvard University Press, 1951), and Emmette S. Redford, *Democracy in the Administrative State* (New York: Oxford University Press, 1969).

6. Harold Seidman, *Politics, Position, and Power* (3rd ed.; New York: Oxford University Press, 1980), chs. 5 and 6.

7. Robert A. Katzman, "Federal Trade Commission," in James Q. Wilson, ed., *The Politics of Regulation* (New York: Basic Books, 1980), pp. 152–187, esp. pp. 166–171.

8. Frederick C. Mosher, *Democracy and the Public Service* (2nd ed.; New York: Oxford University Press, 1982), p. 113.

9. See *ibid.*, pp. 110–142, for a nice summary.

10. *Ibid.*, p. 110.

11. *Ibid.*, pp. 118–119, italics mine.

12. Steven Kelman, "Occupational Safety and Health Administration," in Wilson, ed., *Politics of Regulation*, p. 251.

13. *Ibid.*

14. *Ibid.*, p. 252, italics mine.

15. Herbert Kaufman, *The Administrative Behavior of Federal Bureau Chiefs* (Washington, D.C.: Brookings Institution, 1981), p. 47.

16. Rourke, *Bureaucracy, Politics, and Public Policy*, p. 206.

17. Kelman, "Occupational Safety and Health Administration," p. 251.

18. Seidman, *Politics, Position, and Power*, ch. 6.

19. *Ibid.*

20. *Ibid.*, p. 140.

Chapter 2

1. Richard L. Cole and David A. Caputo, "Presidential Control of the Senior Civil Service: Assessing the Strategies of the Nixon Years," *American Political Science Review* 73 (June 1979): 399.

2. Robert Sherrill, *Why They Call It Politics* (2nd ed.; New York: Harcourt Brace Jovanovich, 1974), p. 4.

3. Hugh Heclo, "Issue Networks and the Executive Establishment," in Anthony King, ed., *The New American Political System* (Washington, D.C.: American Enterprise Institute, 1978), p. 106.

4. *Ibid.*

5. Thomas E. Cronin, "Presidents as Chief Executives," in Rexford G. Tugwell and Thomas E. Cronin, eds., *The Presidency Reappraised* (New York: Praeger, 1974), p. 241.

6. Richard E. Neustadt, *Presidential Power* (New York: John Wiley and Sons, 1960). I used the New American Library Signet edition, p. 22.

7. *Ibid.*

8. Graham T. Allison, *Essence of Decision* (Boston: Little, Brown and Co., 1971), pp. 141–143.

9. Steven Kelman, "Occupational Safety and Health Administration," in James Q. Wilson, ed., *The Politics of Regulation* (New York: Basic Books, 1980), p. 254.

10. Cronin, "Presidents as Chief Executives," p. 237.

11. Francis E. Rourke, *Bureaucracy, Politics, and Public Policy* (2nd ed.; Boston: Little, Brown and Co., 1976), pp. 42–77.

12. Harold Seidman, *Politics, Position, and Power* (3rd ed.; New York: Oxford University Press, 1980), p. 171.

13. James E. Webb, *Space-Age Management* (New York: McGraw-Hill, 1969), p. 128. Harold Seidman makes the same point at considerable length; see Seidman, *Politics, Position, and Power*, pp. 133–139.

14. Unless otherwise noted, the appointments referred to were "absorbed" from mass media reports.

15. Rourke, *Bureaucracy, Politics, and Public Policy*, p. 49.

16. Rogers Morton, Interior Secretary under Richard Nixon, is an obvious exception, but Morton was a former Republican Party Chairman, a member of the House of Representatives, and generally well thought of in Washington.

17. See Seidman, *Politics, Position, and Power*, pp. 138–140.

18. *Congressional Quarterly Weekly Report* 39, No. 5 (Jan. 31, 1981): 221–222.

19. The gentleman in question is William G. Lesher. See *ibid.*

20. *Ibid.*

21. *Congressional Quarterly Weekly Report* 39, No. 12 (March 21, 1981): 568.

22. For a thorough discussion of the subject, see Richard F. Fenno, Jr., *Congressmen in Committees* (Boston: Little, Brown and Co., 1973).

23. The same is true for other committees of the Senate, particularly Interior, Armed Services, Labor, and Finance.

24. Ronald Randall, "Presidential Power versus Bureaucratic Intransigence: The Influence of the Nixon Administration on Welfare Policy," *American Political Science Review* 73 (Sept. 1979): 795–810.

25. *Ibid.*, p. 799.

26. Terry M. Moe, "Control and Feedback in Economic Regulation: The Case of the NLRB," *American Political Science Review* 79 (Dec. 1985): 1094–1116.

27. See Kelman, "Occupational Safety and Health Administration," esp. pp. 238–243.

28. Florence Heffron, *The Administrative Regulatory Process* (New York: Longman, 1983), p. 102.

29. See Stephen J. Wayne, *The Legislative Presidency* (New York: Harper and Row, 1978), pp. 71–100, for a clear, concise description.

30. *Ibid.*, p. 73.

31. This is the title of ch. 3 of Neustadt's *Presidential Power*.

32. Heffron, *The Administrative Regulatory Process*, p. 126.

33. Gilbert Y. Steiner, *The Children's Cause* (Washington, D.C.: Brookings Institution, 1976), pp. 173–174.

34. *The United States Government Manual, 1982/83* (Washington, D.C.: U.S. Government Printing Office, 1982), p. 307.

35. *Donovan v. Dewey*, 452 U.S. 594, 598 (1981).

36. Heffron, *The Administrative Regulatory Process*, p. 377.

37. Seidman, *Politics, Position, and Power*, p. 3.

38. *Ibid.*, p. 125.

39. *Ibid.*, p. 129.

40. President's Message on Reorganization, March 25, 1971, as quoted in *ibid.*, p. 115.

41. *Ibid.*, p. 119.

42. Quoted in Lawrence C. Dodd and Richard L. Schott, *Congress and the Administrative State* (New York: John Wiley and Sons, 1979), p. 342, italics mine.

43. For the history, see Richard Polenberg, *Reorganizing Roosevelt's Government: The Controversy Over Executive Reorganization, 1936–1939* (Cambridge, Mass.: Harvard University Press, 1966).

44. See Dodd and Schott, *Congress and the Administrative State*, pp. 335–336.

45. *INS v. Chadha* 103 S. Ct. 2764 (1983).

46. Dodd and Schott, *Congress and the Administrative State*, pp. 334–335.

47. Randall, "Presidential Power versus Bureaucratic Intransigence," pp. 800–802.

48. Seidman, *Politics, Position, and Power*, ch. 4.

49. Heffron, *The Administrative Regulatory Process*, p. 377.

50. The classic description of the budget process of the 1950's and 1960's was Aaron Wildavsky, *The Politics of the Budgetary Process* (Boston: Little, Brown and Co., 1964). Wildavsky has kept the basic manu-

script intact through four editions with lots of things added on. The fourth, and he says final, was published in 1984.

51. Seidman, *Politics, Position, and Power*, p. 171.

52. Wildavsky, *The Politics of the Budgetary Process*, p. 36.

53. See Richard F. Fenno, Jr., *The Power of the Purse* (Boston: Little, Brown and Co., 1966), p. 478, for a description of Eisenhower's reaction.

54. See the preface and prologue to the fourth edition of Wildavsky, *The Politics of the Budgetary Process*, and the works he cites.

55. Heffron, *The Administrative Regulatory Process*, p. 377.

56. Philip Shabecoff, New York Times News Service editorial, reprinted in the *Stevens Point* (Wis.) *Journal*, Feb. 15, 1986.

Chapter 3

1. Herbert Kaufman, *The Administrative Behavior of Federal Bureau Chiefs* (Washington, D.C.: Brookings Institution, 1981), p. 47.

2. Hugh Heclo, "Issue Networks and the Executive Establishment," in Anthony King, ed., *The New American Political System* (Washington, D.C.: American Enterprise Institute, 1978), pp. 87–124. The passage quoted is on pp. 116–117.

3. Robert Salisbury and Kenneth Shepsle, "Congressional Staff Turnover and the Ties-That-Bind," *American Political Science Review* 75 (June 1981): 381–395.

4. *Ibid.*, See table 9, p. 393.

5. *Ibid.*

6. *Ibid.*, p. 383.

7. Though noted by many, probably the best treatment of the constituency connection is David W. Rohde and Kenneth A. Shepsle, "Committee Assignments," in Robert L. Peabody and Nelson W. Polsby, eds., *New Perspectives on the House of Representatives* (3rd ed.; Chicago: Rand McNally and Co., 1977), pp. 295–323.

8. All of this comes from Michael Barone and Grant Ujifusa, *The Almanac of American Politics, 1986* (Washington, D.C.: National Journal, 1985).

9. See Dennis S. Ippolito and Thomas G. Walker, *Political Parties, Interest Groups, and Public Policy: Group Influence in American Politics* (Englewood Cliffs, N.J.: Prentice-Hall, 1980), pp. 357–358.

10. *Ibid.*, p. 373.

11. *Ibid.*

12. Kaufman, *The Administrative Behavior of Federal Bureau Chiefs*, p. 47.

13. Richard F. Fenno, Jr., *Congressmen in Committees* (Boston: Little, Brown and Co., 1973), p. 1.

14. Lawrence C. Dodd and Richard L. Schott, *Congress and the Administrative State* (New York: John Wiley and Sons, 1979), p. 125, italics mine.

15. *Ibid.*, p. 280.

16. *Ibid.*, p. 157.

17. *Ibid.*

18. *Ibid.*

19. Kaufman, *The Administrative Behavior of Federal Bureau Chiefs*, p. 55.

20. Aaron Wildavsky, *The Politics of the Budgetary Process* (4th ed.; Boston: Little, Brown and Co., 1984), pp. 78–79.

21. Dodd and Schott, *Congress and the Administrative State*, p. 164.

22. *Ibid.*, p. 168.

23. *Ibid.*, pp. 242–243.

24. *Ibid.*, p. 170.

25. Kaufman, *The Administrative Behavior of Federal Bureau Chiefs*, p. 48.

26. *Ibid.*, p. 51.

27. *Ibid.*, p. 50.

28. John R. Johannes, "Executive Reports to Congress," *Journal of Communications* 26, No. 3 (Summer 1976): 55–56.

29. See Morris S. Ogul, *Congress Oversees the Bureaucracy* (Pittsburgh: University of Pittsburgh Press, 1976).

30. Robert M. Stein and James L. Regans, "An Empirical Typology of Congressional Oversight," paper presented to the 1978 Annual Meeting of the Southwestern Political Science Association, Houston, Texas, April 12–15, 1978. See esp. pp. 17–18.

31. Dodd and Schott, *Congress and the Administrative State*, p. 168.

32. Thomas A. Henderson, *Congressional Oversight of Executive Agencies: A Study of the House Committee on Government Operations* (Gainesville, Fla.: University of Florida Press, 1970), pp. 21–22.

33. Dodd and Schott, *Congress and the Administrative State*, p. 168.

34. *Ibid.*, pp. 250–251.

35. *Ibid.*, p. 257.

36. *Ibid.*

37. *Ibid.*, p. 261.

38. Joseph Pois, "The General Accounting Office as a Congressional Resource," in *Congressional Support Agencies: Papers Prepared for the Commission on the Operation of the Senate* (Washington, D.C.: U.S. Government Printing Office, 1976), p. 32.

39. *Ibid.*, pp. 40–41.

40. *Ibid.*, p. 48.

41. See Richard E. Brown, *The General Accounting Office* (Knoxville, Tenn.: University of Tennessee Press, 1970), esp. pp. 77–79.

42. *The United States Government Manual, 1982/83* (Washington, D.C.: U.S. Government Printing Office, 1982), p. 305.

43. *Ibid.*

44. A brief summary is contained in Louis M. Kohlmeier, Jr., *The Regulators: Watchdog Agencies and the Public Interest* (New York: Harper and Row, 1969), pp. 55–56. If you want more, see A. Lee Fritschler, *Smoking and Politics* (2nd ed.; Englewood Cliffs, N.J.: Prentice-Hall, 1975).

45. Quoted in Richard Polenberg, *Reorganizing Roosevelt's Government: The Controversy Over Executive Reorganization, 1936–1939* (Cambridge, Mass.: Harvard University Press, 1966), p. 130.

46. *United States Government Manual, 1982/83*, pp. 304–313.

47. Harold Seidman, *Politics, Position, and Power* (3rd ed.; New York: Oxford University Press, 1980), pp. 47–48.

48. See *ibid.*, chs. 4 and 5, or Dodd and Schott, *Congress and the Administrative State*, pp. 331–348.

49. Quoted in Seidman, *Politics, Position, and Power*, p. 48.

50. *Ibid.*

51. *Ibid.*, p. 53.

52. For a description of the battle, see Kohlmeier, *The Regulators*, pp. 57–60.

53. Wildavsky, *The Politics of the Budgetary Process*, pp. 53–54.

54. Kaufman, *The Administrative Behavior of Federal Bureau Chiefs*, p. 51.

55. Michael Kirst, *Government Without Passing Laws* (Chapel Hill, N.C.: University of North Carolina Press, 1969), esp. pp. 115–116.

56. Florence Heffron, *The Administrative Regulatory Process* (New York: Longman, 1983), p. 109.

57. *Ibid.* For more, see Alan Murray, "House Funding Bill Riders

Become Potent Policy Force," *Congressional Quarterly Weekly Report* 38, No. 44 (Nov. 1, 1980): 3255.

58. Heffron, *The Administrative Regulatory Process*, p. 109.

59. Kirst, *Government Without Passing Laws*, p. 73.

60. Salisbury and Shepsle, "Congressional Staff Turnover," p. 382.

61. *Ibid.*, p. 387.

62. *Ibid.*, p. 384.

63. *Ibid.*, p. 389.

64. Kaufman, *The Administrative Behavior of Federal Bureau Chiefs*, p. 165.

65. For a thorough discussion of this problem, see Robert A. Dahl, *A Preface to Democratic Theory* (Chicago: University of Chicago Press, 1956), ch. 4.

66. Emmette S. Redford, *Democracy in the Administrative State* (New York: Oxford University Press, 1969), p. 18.

67. To get an idea of what I might say, however, see Theodore J. Lowi, *The End of Liberalism* (New York: W. W. Norton and Co., 1969).

Chapter 4

1. Dennis S. Ippolito and Thomas G. Walker, *Political Parties, Interest Groups, and Public Policy: Group Influence in American Politics* (Englewood Cliffs, N.J.: Prentice-Hall, 1980), pp. 373–374.

2. See Richard F. Fenno, Jr., *Congressmen in Committees* (Boston: Little, Brown and Co., 1973), ch. 2.

3. For a good description of the constituency connection, see David W. Rohde and Kenneth A. Shepsle, "Committee Assignments," in Robert L. Peabody and Nelson W. Polsby, eds., *New Perspectives on the House of Representatives* (3rd ed.; Chicago: Rand McNally and Co., 1977), pp. 295–323, esp. pp. 303–307.

4. Ippolito and Walker, *Political Parties, Interest Groups, and Public Policy*, pp. 357–358.

5. Francis E. Rourke, *Bureaucracy, Politics, and Public Policy* (2nd ed.; Boston: Little, Brown and Co., 1976), p. 46.

6. See *American Textile Manufacturers Institute v. Donovan*, 101 S. Ct. 2478 (1981), and *Industrial Union Department v. American Petroleum Institute*, 448 U.S. 607 (1980).

7. Bradley Behrman, "Civil Aeronautics Board," in James Q. Wilson, ed., *The Politics of Regulation* (New York: Basic Books, 1980), pp. 75–120, esp. pp. 78–96.

8. See Louis M. Kohlmeier, Jr., *The Regulators: Watchdog Agencies and the Public Interest* (New York: Harper and Row, 1969), pp. 95–104, or Stephen Chapman, "The ICC and the Truckers," in Charles Peters and Michael Nelson, eds., *The Culture of Bureaucracy* (New York: Holt, Rinehart and Winston, 1979), pp. 156–164, esp. pp. 159–160.

9. Marver H. Bernstein, *Regulating Business by Independent Commission* (Princeton, N.J.: Princeton University Press, 1955).

10. See *Moss v. Civil Aeronautics Board* 430 F. 2d 891 (1970).

11. Behrman, "Civil Aeronautics Board," pp. 96–120.

12. James Q. Wilson, "The Politics of Regulation," in Wilson, ed., *Politics of Regulation*, pp. 357–394.

13. Kohlmeier, *The Regulators*, pp. 105–128.

14. Steven Kelman, "Occupational Safety and Health Administration," in Wilson, ed., *Politics of Regulation*, pp. 236–266.

15. *Ibid.*, pp. 252–253.

16. *Ibid.*, p. 253.

17. Herbert Kaufman, *The Administrative Behavior of Federal Bureau Chiefs* (Washington, D.C.: Brookings Institution, 1981), p. 68.

18. *Ibid.*, p. 70.

19. Frederick C. Mosher, *Democracy and the Public Service* (2nd ed.; New York: Oxford University Press, 1982), p. 122.

20. *Ibid.*, p. 139.

21. Kaufman, *The Administrative Behavior of Federal Bureau Chiefs*, p. 151.

22. Bob Kuttner, "The Social Security Hysteria," *New Republic*, Dec. 27, 1982, pp. 17–21.

23. Kaufman, *The Administrative Behavior of Federal Bureau Chiefs*, p. 69.

24. *Ibid.*, pp. 69–70, italics mine.

25. See Wilson, "Politics of Regulation," pp. 357–394.

26. Kaufman, *The Administrative Behavior of Federal Bureau Chiefs*, p. 76.

27. Norman J. Ornstein and Shirley Elder, *Interest Groups, Lobbying and Policy Making* (Washington, D.C.: Congressional Quarterly Press, 1978), p. 47.

28. *Ibid.*, p. 48.

29. Kaufman, *The Administrative Behavior of Federal Bureau Chiefs*, pp. 68–69.

30. Eisenhower allowed little organized labor input into his Labor Department selections and Ronald Reagan did the same, plus making some appointments at the Department of Education that were unpopular with its clientele groups, but most Presidents just leave well enough alone, and even these two hardly made non-clientele appointments a habit.

31. Kaufman, *The Administrative Behavior of Federal Bureau Chiefs*, pp. 68–69.

32. For a brief discussion of lobbying the bureaucracy, see Ippolito and Walker, *Political Parties, Interest Groups, and Public Policy*, pp. 390–399.

33. Rourke, *Bureaucracy, Politics, and Public Policy*, p. 46.

34. Harold Seidman, *Politics, Position, and Power* (3rd ed.; New York: Oxford University Press, 1980), p. 284.

35. David B. Truman, *The Governmental Process* (New York: Alfred A. Knopf, 1964), p. 461, quoted in Seidman, *Politics, Position, and Power*, p. 279.

36. Seidman, *Politics, Position, and Power*, p. 279.

37. On the role of these farmer-elected committees, see Randall B. Ripley and Grace A. Franklin, *Congress, the Bureaucracy, and Public Policy* (Homewood, Ill.: Dorsey Press, 1976), pp. 76–79, or Theodore J. Lowi, "How the Farmers Get What They Want," in Theodore J. Lowi and Randall B. Ripley, eds., *Legislative Politics U.S.A.* (3rd ed.; Boston: Little, Brown and Co., 1973), pp. 184–191. The quote is from Lowi, p. 187.

38. Lowi, "How the Farmers Get What They Want," p. 187.

39. Seidman, *Politics, Position, and Power*, p. 254.

40. *Ibid.*

41. *Ibid.*

42. Associated Press, "Wilkinson Quits Post," reprinted in the *Stevens Point* (Wis.) *Journal*, March 17, 1986.

43. See Phillip O. Foss, *Politics and Grass* (Seattle: University of Washington Press, 1960).

44. See "Dairy Support Changes OK'd," *Milwaukee Sentinel*, Aug. 11, 1982, pp. 1 and 12.

Chapter 5

1. *Sierra Club v. Morton*, 405 U.S. 727 (1972). This initial challenge was dismissed when the Sierra Club was held to lack standing. The delay, however, eventually proved fatal to the resort.

2. *Citizens to Preserve Overton Park v. Volpe*, 401 U.S. 402, 415 *et seq.* (1971).

3. *American Textile Manufacturers Institute v. Donovan*, 101 S. Ct. 2478 (1981).

4. *Industrial Union Department v. American Petroleum Institute*, 448 U.S. 607 (1980).

5. Florence Heffron, *The Administrative Regulatory Process* (New York: Longman, 1983), p. 295.

6. *DeFunis v. Odegaard*, 416 U.S. 312 (1974). That cleared the way for *Bakke v. Regents of the University of California*, 438 U.S. 265 (1978).

7. *Sierra Club v. Morton.*

8. John Marshall Harlan, in *Abbott Laboratories, Inc. v. Gardner*, 387 U.S. 136 (1967).

9. Heffron, *The Administrative Regulatory Process*, p. 295.

10. *Harmon v. Bruckner*, 355 U.S. 579 (1958), and *Oestereich v. Selective Service System Board No. 11*, 393 U.S. 233 (1968).

11. *United States v. Students Challenging Regulatory Agency Procedures*, 412 U.S. 669 (1973).

12. Heffron, *The Administrative Regulatory Process*, p. 314.

13. *Industrial Union Department v. API*, quoted in Leif H. Carter, *Administrative Law and Politics* (Boston: Little, Brown and Co., 1983), p. 90.

14. Heffron, *The Administrative Regulatory Process*, p. 314.

15. *Ibid.*, pp. 129–130.

16. William Rehnquist, in *Vermont Yankee Nuclear Power Corp. v. Natural Resources Defense Council, Inc.*, 435 U.S. 519, 549 *et seq.* (1978).

17. *Goldberg v. Kelly*, 397 U.S. 254 (1970).

18. *Ibid.*

19. For example, in *Goss v. Lopez*, 419 U.S. 565 (1975), the Court required a hearing before students could be suspended for disciplinary reasons, but the hearing was an informal one indeed compared to the one ordered in *Goldberg v. Kelly*. In *Board of Curators of the University of Missouri et al. v. Horowitz*, 435 U.S. 78 (1978), however, the Court held

that no hearing was required at all to dismiss a student for academic reasons.

20. *Federal Crop Insurance Corp. v. Merrill*, 332 U.S. 380 (1947).

21. Heffron, *The Administrative Regulatory Process*, pp. 204–205.

22. *Federal Crop Insurance Corp. v. Merrill.*

23. Quoted in Carter, *Administrative Law and Politics*, p. 177.

24. *Ibid.*, p. 129.

25. Paul Verkuil, "A Study of Informal Adjudication Procedures," *University of Chicago Law Review* 739 (1976): 757–771, reprinted in Carter, *Administrative Law and Politics*, pp. 124–129. All citations are to the edited version in Carter. See p. 125.

26. *Ibid.*, p. 127.

27. Heffron, *The Administrative Regulatory Process*, p. 236.

28. *Ibid.*, p. 242.

29. *Ibid.*, p. 241.

30. *ACT v. FCC*, F.2d 458, 477 (D.C. Cir. 1977). It is discussed in Heffron, *The Administrative Regulatory Process*, pp. 241–243.

31. See Heffron, *The Administrative Regulatory Process*, pp. 235–236.

32. Verkuil, "Study of Informal Adjudication Procedures," p. 125.

33. *Association of National Advertisers v. FTC*, 627 F.2d 1151, 1174 (D.C. Cir. 1979).

34. *Cindarella Career and Finishing Schools, Inc. v. FTC*, 425 F.2d 583 (D.C. Cir. 1970). The case is discussed in Carter, *Administrative Law and Politics*, pp. 164–167.

35. Heffron, *The Administrative Regulatory Process*, pp. 243–244.

36. Quoted in *ibid.*, p. 244.

37. *Ibid.*

38. See Carter, *Administrative Law and Politics*, pp. 162–164.

39. Verkuil, "Study of Informal Adjudication Procedures," p. 125.

40. Heffron, *The Administrative Regulatory Process*, pp. 269–270.

41. *Federal Crop Insurance Corp. v. Merrill.* The passage quoted was in his dissent. See Carter, *Administrative Law and Politics*, p. 139.

42. Verkuil, "Study of Informal Adjudication Procedures," p. 125.

43. Heffron, *The Administrative Regulatory Process*, pp. 271–272.

44. *Dunlop v. Bachowski*, 421 U.S. 560, 577 (1975), quoted in *ibid.*, p. 313, italics mine.

45. *National Welfare Rights Organization v. Mathews*, 533 F.2d 637, 648 (D.C. Cir. 1976), quoted in *ibid.*, pp. 311–312, italics mine.

46. The cases were *Office of Communication, United Church of Christ v. FCC*, 359 F.2d 994 (D.C. Cir. 1966), *Morton v. Ruiz*, 415 U.S. 199, 231–236 (1974), and *National Welfare Rights*, respectively.

47. *National Welfare Rights*, quoted in Heffron, *The Administrative Regulatory Process*, p. 313.

Chapter 6

1. Arthur Maass, *Muddy Waters:: The Army Engineers and the Nation's Rivers* (Cambridge, Mass.: Harvard University Press, 1951).

2. "Senate Water-Use Bill Pits Big Firms Against Small Farms," *Congressional Quarterly Weekly Report* 37, No. 39 (Sept. 29, 1979): 2123.

3. *Ibid.*, p. 2125.

4. Francis E. Rourke, *Bureaucracy, Politics, and Public Policy* (3rd ed.; Boston: Little, Brown and Co., 1984), p. 4.

5. Frederick C. Mosher, *Democracy and the Public Service* (2nd ed.; New York: Oxford University Press, 1982), p. 118.

6. Hugh Heclo, "Issue Networks and the Executive Establishment," in Anthony King, ed., *The New American Political System* (Washington, D.C.: American Enterprise Institute, 1978), p. 123.

7. Harold Seidman, *Politics, Position, and Power* (3rd ed.; New York: Oxford University Press, 1980), p. 154.

8. *Ibid.*, p. 155.

9. *Ibid.*

10. Harold J. Laski, "The Limitations of the Expert," *Harpers*, Dec. 1930, quoted in O. Glenn Stahl, *Public Personnel Administration* (7th ed.; New York: Harper and Row, 1976), pp. 274–275.

Bibliography

Aberbach, Joel D., and Bert A. Rockman. "Clashing Beliefs Within the Executive Branch: The Nixon Administration Bureaucracy." *American Political Science Review* 70 (June 1976): 456-468.

Allison, Graham T. *Essence of Decision.* Boston: Little, Brown and Co., 1971.

Appleby, Paul H. *Morality and Administration in Democratic Government.* Baton Rouge, La.: Louisiana State University Press, 1952.

Barone, Michael, and Grant Ujifusa. *The Almanac of American Politics, 1986.* Washington, D.C.: National Journal, 1985.

Behrman, Bradley. "Civil Aeronautics Board." In James Q. Wilson, ed., *The Politics of Regulation,* pp. 75-120. New York: Basic Books, 1980.

Bernstein, Marver H. *Regulating Business by Independent Commission.* Princeton, N.J.: Princeton University Press, 1955.

Berry, Jeffrey. *Lobbying for the People.* Princeton, N.J.: Princeton University Press, 1977.

Branch, Taylor. "Courage Without Esteem: Profiles in Whistle Blowing." In Charles Peters and Michael Nelson, eds., *The Culture of Bureaucracy,* pp. 217-237. New York: Holt, Rinehart and Winston, 1979.

Brown, Richard E. *The General Accounting Office.* Knoxville, Tenn.: University of Tennessee Press, 1970.

Carson, Rachel. *Silent Spring.* Boston: Houghton Mifflin, 1962.

Carter, Leif H. *Administrative Law and Politics.* Boston: Little, Brown and Co., 1983.

Cater, Douglass. *Power in Washington*. New York: Vintage Books, 1964.

Cayer, N. Joseph. *Managing Human Resources*. New York: St. Martin's Press, 1980.

Chapman, Stephen. "The ICC and the Truckers." In Charles Peters and Michael Nelson, eds., *The Culture of Bureaucracy*, pp. 156–164. New York: Holt, Rinehart and Winston, 1979.

Cole, Richard L., and David A. Caputo. "Presidential Control of the Senior Civil Service: Assessing the Strategies of the Nixon Years." *American Political Science Review* 73 (June 1979): 399–413.

Congressional Quarterly Weekly Report. Vol. 39, No. 5 (Jan. 31, 1981).

———. Vol. 39, No. 12 (March 21, 1981).

———. Vol. 39, No. 27 (July 4, 1981).

Cronin, Thomas E. "Presidents as Chief Executives." In Rexford G. Tugwell and Thomas E. Cronin, eds., *The Presidency Reappraised*, pp. 234–266. New York: Praeger, 1974.

Dahl, Robert A. *A Preface to Democratic Theory*. Chicago: University of Chicago Press, 1956.

Davis, David Howard. *Energy Politics*. 3rd ed. New York: St. Martin's Press, 1982.

Dodd, Lawrence C., and Richard L. Schott. *Congress and the Administrative State*. New York: John Wiley and Sons, 1979.

Fenno, Richard F., Jr. *Congressmen in Committees*. Boston: Little, Brown and Co., 1973.

———. *The Power of the Purse*. Boston: Little, Brown and Co., 1966.

Finer, Herman. "Administrative Responsibility in Democratic Government." *Public Administration Review* 2 (Summer 1941): 335–350. Reprinted in Francis E. Rourke, *Bureaucratic Power in National Politics* (3rd ed.; Boston: Little, Brown and Co., 1978).

Fiorina, Morris P. "The Case of the Vanishing Marginals: The Bureaucracy Did It." *American Political Science Review* 71 (March 1977): 177–181.

Foss, Phillip O. *Politics and Grass*. Seattle: University of Washington Press, 1960.

Fox, Harrison W., Jr., and Susan Webb Hammond. *Congressional Staffs: The Invisible Force in American Lawmaking*. Glencoe, Ill.: Free Press, 1977.

Freeman, J. Leiper. *The Political Process: Executive Bureau–Legislative Relations*. New York: Random House, 1955.

Friedrich, Carl J. "Public Policy and the Nature of Administrative Responsibility." *Public Policy* 1 (1940): 3–24. Reprinted in Francis E. Rourke, *Bureaucratic Power in National Politics* (3rd ed.; Boston: Little, Brown and Co., 1978).

Fritschler, A. Lee. *Smoking and Politics*. 2nd ed. Englewood Cliffs, N.J.: Prentice-Hall, 1975.

Gelhorn, Walter. *When Americans Complain*. Cambridge, Mass.: Harvard University Press, 1966.

Goulden, Joseph C. *The Superlawyers*. New York: Dell Publishing Co., 1971.

Green, Mark. "The Gang That Can't Deregulate." *New Republic*, March 21, 1983, pp. 14–17.

Grimes, Alan Pendleton. *American Political Thought*. Rev. ed. Hinsdale, Ill.: Dryden Press, 1960.

Harris, Joseph. *Congressional Control of Administration*. Washington, D.C.: Brookings Institution, 1964.

Heclo, Hugh. *A Government of Strangers: Executive Politics in Washington*. Washington, D.C.: Brookings Institution, 1977.

———. "Issue Networks and the Executive Establishment." In Anthony King, ed., *The New American Political System*, pp. 87–124. Washington, D.C.: American Enterprise Institute, 1978.

Heffron, Florence. *The Administrative Regulatory Process*. New York: Longman, 1983.

Henderson, Thomas A. *Congressional Oversight of Executive Agencies: A Study of the House Committee on Government Operations*. Gainesville, Fla.: University of Florida Press, 1970.

Ippolito, Dennis S., and Thomas G. Walker. *Political Parties, Interest Groups, and Public Policy: Group Influence in American Politics*. Englewood Cliffs, N.J.: Prentice-Hall, 1980.

Johannes, John R. "Executive Reports to Congress." *Journal of Communications* 26, No. 3 (Summer 1976): 53–61.

Katzman, Robert A. "Federal Trade Commission." In James Q. Wilson, ed., *The Politics of Regulation*, pp. 152–187. New York: Basic Books, 1980.

Kaufman, Herbert. *The Administrative Behavior of Federal Bureau Chiefs*. Washington, D.C.: Brookings Institution, 1981.

Kelman, Steven. "Occupational Safety and Health Administration." In James Q. Wilson, ed., *The Politics of Regulation*, pp. 236–266. New York: Basic Books, 1980.

Kendall, Willmoore, and George W. Carey. "The Intensity Problem and

Democratic Theory." *American Political Science Review* 62 (March 1968): 5–24.

Kirst, Michael. *Government Without Passing Laws.* Chapel Hill, N.C.: University of North Carolina Press, 1969.

Kohlmeier, Louis M., Jr. *The Regulators: Watchdog Agencies and the Public Interest.* New York: Harper and Row, 1969.

Kuttner, Bob. "The Social Security Hysteria." *New Republic,* Dec. 27, 1982, pp. 17–21.

Lowi, Theodore J. *The End of Liberalism.* New York: W. W. Norton and Co., 1969.

———. "How the Farmers Get What They Want." In Theodore J. Lowi and Randall B. Ripley, eds., *Legislative Politics U.S.A.,* pp. 184–191. 3rd ed. Boston: Little, Brown and Co., 1973.

Maass, Arthur. *Muddy Waters: The Army Engineers and the Nation's Rivers.* Cambridge, Mass.: Harvard University Press, 1951.

Moe, Terry M. "Control and Feedback in Economic Regulation: The Case of the NLRB." *American Political Science Review* 79 (Dec. 1985): 1094–1116.

Mosher, Frederick C. *Democracy and the Public Service.* 2nd ed. New York: Oxford University Press, 1982.

Neustadt, Richard E. *Presidential Power.* New York: John Wiley and Sons, 1960.

Ogul, Morris S. *Congress Oversees the Bureaucracy.* Pittsburgh: University of Pittsburgh Press, 1976.

Ornstein, Norman J., and Shirley Elder. *Interest Groups, Lobbying and Policy Making.* Washington, D.C.: Congressional Quarterly Press, 1978.

Pois, Joseph. "The General Accounting Office as a Congressional Resource." In *Congressional Support Agencies, Papers Prepared for the Commission on the Operation of the Senate.* Washington, D.C.: U.S. Government Printing Office, 1976.

Polenberg, Richard. *Reorganizing Roosevelt's Government: The Controversy Over Executive Reorganization, 1936–1939.* Cambridge, Mass.: Harvard University Press, 1966.

President's Committee on Administrative Management. *Report of the Committee with Special Studies.* Washington, D.C.: U.S. Government Printing Office, 1937.

Randall, Ronald. "Presidential Power versus Bureaucratic Intransigence:

The Influence of the Nixon Administration on Welfare Policy." *American Political Science Review* 73 (Sept. 1979): 795–810.

Redford, Emmette S. *Democracy in the Administrative State.* New York: Oxford University Press, 1969.

Riker, William H. *Democracy in the United States.* 2nd ed. New York: Macmillan, 1965.

Ripley, Randall B., and Grace A. Franklin. *Congress, the Bureaucracy, and Public Policy.* Homewood, Ill.: Dorsey Press, 1976.

Risser, James. "The U.S. Forest Service: Smokey's Strip Miners." In Charles Peters and Michael Nelson, eds., *The Culture of Bureaucracy,* pp. 146–156. New York: Holt, Rinehart and Winston, 1979.

Rohde, David W., and Kenneth A. Shepsle. "Committee Assignments." In Robert L. Peabody and Nelson W. Polsby, eds., *New Perspectives on the House of Representatives,* pp. 295–323. 3rd ed. Chicago: Rand McNally and Co., 1977.

Rourke, Francis E. *Bureaucracy, Politics, and Public Policy.* 2nd ed. Boston: Little, Brown and Co., 1976.

Salisbury, Robert, and Kenneth Shepsle. "Congressional Staff Turnover and the Ties-That-Bind." *American Political Science Review* 75 (June 1981): 381–395.

Seidman, Harold. *Politics, Position, and Power.* 3rd ed. New York: Oxford University Press, 1980.

"Senate Water-Use Bill Pits Big Firms Against Small Farms." *Congressional Quarterly Weekly Report* 37, No. 39 (Sept. 29, 1979): 2121–2133.

Shapiro, Martin. "On Predicting the Future of Administrative Law." *Regulation* 6, No. 3 (May/June 1982): 18–25.

Sherrill, Robert. *Why They Call It Politics.* 2nd ed. New York: Harcourt Brace Jovanovich, 1974.

Stahl, O. Glenn. *Public Personnel Administration.* 7th ed. New York: Harper and Row, 1976.

Steiner, Gilbert Y. *The Children's Cause.* Washington, D.C.: Brookings Institution, 1976.

Truman, David B. *The Governmental Process.* New York: Alfred A. Knopf, 1964.

Tugwell, Rexford G., and Thomas E. Cronin, eds. *The Presidency Reappraised.* New York: Praeger, 1974.

Verkuil, Paul. "A Study of Informal Adjudication Procedures." *University of Chicago Law Review* 739 (1976): 757–771.

Wayne, Stephen J. *The Legislative Presidency*. New York: Harper and Row, 1978.

Webb, James E. *Space-Age Management*. New York: McGraw-Hill, 1969.

Wildavsky, Aaron. *The Politics of the Budgetary Process*. 4th ed. Boston: Little, Brown and Co., 1984.

Wilson, James Q. "The Politics of Regulation." In James Q. Wilson, ed., *The Politics of Regulation*, pp. 357–394. New York: Basic Books, 1980.

Worrell, Albert C. *Principles of Forest Policy*. New York: McGraw-Hill, 1970.

Index